CELEBRATION OF THE SEAS

OF THE

HERITAGE FOR THE FUTURE

CELEBRATION OF THE SEAS

HERITAGE FOR THE FUTURE

PATRICIO ROBLES GIL • PABLO CERVANTES

PRESENTATION
JOSÉ TORRES CAMPOS

FOREWORD
ERNESTO AMTMANN

CEMEX

The sea: to contemplate the hypnotic force of its waves, to feel in its breeze the freshness of its very life and to realize that our existence is possible only because we are at a precise distance from a star that creates the necessary temperature conditions so that the waters of the seas can exist in a liquid state throughout the planet.

Thanks to that "accident of fortune," the miracle of life occurred on Earth. Oceans cover three quarters of its surface in a continuous fashion, and constitute the most important pillar of our biological resources. Besides stabilizing the atmosphere and causing many climatic phenomena, day to day the moisture of the seas nourishes our dry continents.

The wealth of the seas has served as a source of food for humankind for thousands of years, but today we have come to realize that the immensity of their resources has a limit, and that the pressure we have exerted upon them has upset the balance of the natural order.

In an attempt to better understand the importance of the role that the oceans play in the life of humankind, the United Nations has declared 1998 the International Year of the Ocean. Cemex joins in this endeavor and presents *Celebration of the Seas: Heritage for the Future.*

For humans, the seas of the world represent a symbol of freedom and of the majesty of life itself. That is why we have invited several different authors to participate in this book, uniting them in a celebration of the seas, within the framework of the last major world exposition of this century: Expo '98, to be held in Lisbon.

The words and images of these contributors coincide in one respect: the future of humankind depends on the health of the oceans. Without this lung, without this soul on Earth, life simply would not be possible. The sea is so important for many of these authors that several agree on this point: instead of being called Earth, our world should be called Planet Ocean.

Cemex

"To swim fishlike, horizontally, was the logical method in a medium eight hundred times denser than air.

To halt and hang attached to nothing, no lines or air pipe to the surface, was a dream."

Excerpted from *The Silent World* by Jacques-Yves Cousteau with Frédéric Dumas, New York, Harper Collins Publishers, Inc., 1953.

To the memory of Jacques-Yves Cousteau, who made it possible to fulfill that dream, and Ramón Bravo,
who was joined to him in life with his images. Both of them opened up our eyes to conservation of the seas.

With great respect for all those who have departed, leaving us their example to continue to disseminate what for many is unknown.
Accompanying them are women and men from many countries, photographers and authors of this book, to celebrate the seas:

DOUG ALLAN, MIKE BACON, DES & JEN BARTLETT, FRED BAVENDAM, PAUL BERGER, GEORGIENNE E. BRADLEY, JIM BRANDENBURG,

ALDO BRANDO, HOWARD BUFFETT, NICK CALOYIANIS, TOM CAMPBELL, JOHN CANCALOSI, PABLO CERVANTES, BRANDON D. COLE, CLAUDIO CONTRERAS,

BEN & LYNN CROPP, MIKE CRUISE, BILL CURTSINGER, CHUCK DAVIS, TUI DE ROY, DAVID DOUBILET, STEVE DROGIN, JACK DYKINGA, SYLVIA A. EARLE,

FULVIO ECCARDI, CHRISTINE ECKSTROM, GERRY ELLIS, CARLOS EYLES, DAVID B. FLEETHAM, JEFF FOOTT, KATHRYN S. FULLER, JOE GALKOWSKI,

KENNETH GARRETT, MICHELLE GILDERS, FRANÇOIS GOHIER, MICHAEL GORE, HOWARD HALL, MICHELE B. HALL, RICHARD HERRMANN,

THOR HEYERDAHL, JUAN HIDALGO, MARTHA HILL, FERNANDO HOLSCHNEIDER, GEORGE H.H. HUEY, JOHN HYDE, JAY IRELAND,

MITSUAKI IWAGO, MIKE JOHNSON, BURT JONES, RYUKICHI KAMEDA, JEAN-MARC LA ROQUE, FRANS LANTING, PAT & TOM LEESON,

CANDY LOPESINO, WAYNE LYNCH, MARYLOU MCCRAY, JOE MCDONALD, THOMAS D. MANGELSEN, FRANCISCO MÁRQUEZ, TONY MARTIN,

DAVID MUENCH, WILLIAM NEILL, CHRISTOPHER NEWBERT, FLIP NICKLIN, D. PARER, E. PARER-COOK, DOUG PERRINE, DIETER & MARY PLAGE,

JASON PUDDIFOOT, HANS REINHARD, GRAHAM ROBERTSON, PATRICIO ROBLES GIL, NORBERT ROSING, JASMINE ROSSI, KEVIN SCHAFER,

MIKE SEVERNS, JOHN SHAW, MAURINE SHIMLOCK, MICHAEL SMALL, WINLAND SMITH, JORGE SOBERÓN, JEREMY STAFFORD-DEITSCH, ROGER STEENE,

BOB TALBOT, JOSEPH VAN OS, MARK VAN PUTTEN, ENRIQUETA VELARDE, STANTON A. WATERMAN, JAMES D. WATT, RICHARD WEBER,

F. STUART WESTMORLAND, DOC WHITE, STAFFAN WIDSTRAND, BIRGITTE WILMS, ART WOLFE, KONRAD WOTHE, NORBERT WU, GÜNTER ZIESLER.

PRODUCTION
Agrupación Sierra Madre, S.C.
Redacta, S.A. de C.V.

EDITORIAL DIRECTION
Antonio Bolívar

GENERAL COORDINATION
Eugenia Pallares

GRAPHIC DESIGN
AND PHOTO EDITING
Patricio Robles Gil
Pablo Cervantes
Juan Carlos Burgoa
Yvonne Udaeta

TYPESETTING
Socorro Gutiérrez
Patricia Zepeda
Federico Mozo
Rocío Moreno

PREPRESS LIAISON
Ignacio Narro

EDITORIAL SUPPORT
María Luisa Madrazo
Elena León
Georgina Ferrer
Blanca Luz Pulido

PRINTING & BOUNDING LIAISON
Turner Libros, S.A.
Madrid

EDITORIAL REVISION,
TRANSLATION, AND PROOFREADING
Susan B. Kapilian

PRINTED BY
Artes Gráficas Palermo, S.L.
Madrid

First English edition, 1998
Copyright of this edition is the property of CEMEX, S.A. de C.V.

Copyright 1998, Agrupación Sierra Madre, S.C.
Prado Norte 324, 11000 Mexico City.

ISBN 968-6397-52-3
D. L.: M.-20.401-1998

ACKNOWLEDGMENTS

Aeroméxico, Baja Expeditions, Dorado Divers, Exportadora de Sal, North American Nature Photography Association,
Reserva de la Biósfera El Vizcaíno, Scuba Du, Secretaría de Medio Ambiente, Recursos Naturales y Pesca, Telmex

Shelton P. Applegate, Joaquín Ardura, Alfonso Arnold, Inés Arroyo, Amelia Bolívar, Juan Ignacio Bremer, Alan Broder, José Esteban Calderón, Javier Cervantes, Cecilia Chávez Peón, Dalia Conde, Coleen Cook, Luis Espinosa Arrubarrena, Stephen B. Freligh, Martín García Urtiaga, Mónica Gutiérrez, Julián Hernández, Andrea Huerta, Carlos Manterola, Montserrat Martínez, Karla Mellado, María Asunción E. de Migoya, Aarón y Margarita Navarrete, Aldi de Oyarzábal, Raúl Pérez Madero, Patricia Rojo, Víctor Sánchez, Manuel Senderos, Michael Small

Cover: Humpback whale breaching. Chatham Strait, Alaska, USA. © **Thomas D. Mangelsen**; *page 2:* Pacific manta ray. Socorro Island, Mexico © **François Gohier**/Auscape;
page 4: Breaking wave. Oahu, Hawaii, USA. © **Paul Berger**/Tony Stone Images/Mexico; *page 6:* Polar bear mother with cubs at a clearing storm. Wapusk National Park, Manitoba, Canada. © **Thomas D. Mangelsen**;
page 10: Great Barrier Reef Marine Park. Australia. © **D. Parer** & **E. Parer-Cook**/Auscape; *page 12:* Gray whale calf. Ojo de Liebre Lagoon, Baja California Sur, Mexico. © **Howard Buffett**;
page 14: The Arch. Los Cabos, Baja California Sur, Mexico. © **Patricio Robles Gil**/Sierra Madre; *page 17:* Falkland steamer duck. Falkland Islands, UK. © **Patricio Robles Gil**/Sierra Madre

...God wanted the Earth to be one, united, and no longer separated, by the sea...

And all of a sudden, the entire Earth emerged round as a ball from the deep blue...

FERNANDO PESSOA

I am most pleased to present this beautiful book, proposed by commissioner Ernesto Amtmann, responsible for Mexico's participation in the Lisbon World Exposition, Expo '98, which deserves recognition for the level of quality it will attain.

The theme of Expo '98 is "The Oceans: A Heritage for the Future." One of its intentions is to commemorate the past, focussing attention on the ocean voyages made by the Portuguese navigator Vasco da Gama from Lisbon to India, by way of Africa, five hundred years ago. However, the major aim of the exposition is to protect in the future the message that has come to us from the past: that oceans are a feature uniting different civilizations; in other words, oceans are a symbol of the physical dimension of humankind.

Thus, Expo '98 is undoubtedly oriented toward the future. In the new international context of globalization and interdependence, it will serve as a real forum for reflections about the role of the oceans in policies for sustained and sustainable development, a veritable parliament to examine the way in which we should deal with our planet's liquid element in the coming millennium.

The international community has supported this undertaking most eloquently. We have over 150 official participants, including countries and international organizations, all of whose contributions are outstanding.

We are also fortunate to have the sponsorship of the United Nations which, through its General Assembly and in keeping with a proposal made by Portugal, declared 1998 the International Year of the Ocean.

We believe that it is extremely significant that in Lisbon, in this World Exposition in which the great majority of the international community is participating, countries with different dimensions and degrees of development have made the commitment to discuss the safeguarding and protection of our oceans and their resources, and to see to it that this conservation is an essential goal we must achieve.

The importance of the sea not only resides in the fact that it produces most of the oxygen on this planet and that from it are extracted one hundred million tons of food for humans each year. The sea is the foremost source of life, in it are represented all the taxonomic groups that exist on this planet and, although hundreds of thousands of the species that dwell in it are known, the great majority of them are still a mystery for us.

The sea brings us together. It is a meeting place for continents and for people; it is also the point around which the planet's global commitment should center. Celebrating this encounter is the purpose of this book, an undertaking of one of the countries that is privileged thanks to its contact with two major oceans: Mexico.

Celebration of the Seas: Heritage for the Future is an important work for many reasons, mainly because it is the book commemorating the Lisbon World Exposition —Expo '98—, but also in view of the fact that it brings together different visions of men and women, writers and photographers from many countries who have made the sea a way of life, and who share with us the beauty of the marine realm, but their concern for its problems as well.

This book is also the testimony of the enthusiastic participation of different sectors of society committed to the conservation of our natural heritage. CEMEX, a company that has distinguished itself through its efforts to disseminate knowledge related to biodiversity, and the support it has given to projects aimed at its conservation, once again sets an example to be followed with the publication of this book.

Celebration of the Seas joins us in the aesthetic emotion afforded by the oceans: each image celebrates beauty, harmony, and life, and links us together in the responsibility to conserve our oceans, an essential element for the continued existence of our planet.

Like this book, the sea unites us. Now our obligation is to make that union a task for the present, and for the future.

JOSÉ TORRES CAMPOS
Commissioner-General
Lisbon Expo '98

From pre-Hispanic times, Mexico has been a privileged land. Nature gave this country one of the widest ranges of climates, landscapes, and flora and fauna on this planet. Reflected in the great diversity of its natural resources is the variety of its environments, and the amalgamation of its historical roots has led to its extraordinary cultural wealth.

Mexico, with over eleven thousand kilometers of littorals, practically surrounded by seas, between the Atlantic and Pacific Oceans, has one of the most important marine diversities on Earth. The natural abundance and beauty of the Gulf of California and the Mexican Caribbean are an example of this.

Its seas, patrimony of humankind, constitute a fundamental objective of ambitious research programs, in which cooperation models and efforts are combined.

The influence of the oceans has been decisive for many civilizations in the past, and will continue to be so in the future. Mexico, with its pavilion at the Lisbon World Exposition, seeks not only to present its exceptional marine wealth and age-old relationship between humans and nature, but also to maintain its leadership in promoting and initiating programs geared to protecting marine ecosystems, such as decreeing the permanent prohibition to capture sea turtles, the protection of gray whales, and the clear definition of the limits of its territorial seas, as well as to propose ideas, solutions, and alternatives for contemporary problems.

We need to continue to carry out actions that enhance our knowledge of the marine world and all its creatures, for that is how we can admire and respect this environment, and thus exploit the oceans in a rational and sustainable way.

That is why we decided to propose the publication of this book to CEMEX, a company that was born in Mexico and has been internationalized, becoming one of the leading firms in its field, but most importantly because it is a leader in the dissemination of our planet's biodiversity. For several years now, along with Agrupación Sierra Madre, it has done outstanding work in the field of publishing which is acknowledged worldwide in the area of works on nature.

This book is another example of an initiative taken by Mexico and of its participation in Expo '98. Through its texts and images, it strives to make known the beauty of marine flora and fauna, which account for more than 90% of the Earth's biosphere.

Celebration of the Seas: Heritage for the Future, with its spectacular photography, hopes to invite readers to begin to taste the exciting marine life that surrounds us.

If this book manages to touch the hearts of its readers, if it awakens interest in gaining further knowledge, and if it encourages activities fostering the future of the oceans, we will be satisfied. We will have achieved our objective so that this universe of organisms and beings continues to fulfill its function in our world's complex system of life.

ERNESTO AMTMANN
Commissioner-General of Mexico
Lisbon Expo '98

Life appeared on this planet over 3 500 million years ago; and it began in the sea, where the conditions necessary for the existence of the first organisms were present. For that reason, from the standpoint of the evolution of life in our world, humankind has just come onto the scene.

We haven't changed much since our origins and yet our presence has drastically modified the world in which we live. Nowadays, the daily activities of millions of people are having a profound impact on biotic resources, thus altering the natural order which sustains the human species.

We can view our planet as an immense organism that is held together without interruptions by the seas, which give it life. Everything is interrelated: the changes we effect in the natural world have a cost and a benefit. Whether we make intelligent use of the resources of the seas depends on our wisdom in this regard.

Just fifty years ago, most of the oceans were considered pristine. Now, although we have explored many parts of the seas, we are barely starting to discover the enormous potential they contain.

In Mexico, local fishermen on the Gulf of California know, every year, by the success of their catches, whether there was a lot of snow that winter in the Rocky Mountains in Colorado, U.S., more than a thousand kilometers away from the northern extreme of the Gulf. The reason is very simple: the Colorado River springs from the heart of those mountains, and its volume increases when the snow melts, carrying nutrients towards its mouth in the Gulf of California, nutrients that enrich its waters and lead to greater productivity. Unfortunately, the reason the fishermen can tell when a particular year has had considerable snowfall is because all along the course of the river, there are various dams that irrigate the southwestern U.S., thus curbing its natural flow and that of its nutrients, causing the Colorado River to arrive with less force or almost dry at its mouth. Only during exceptional years the locks of the dams are opened and the river can pour its waters into the Gulf of California.

This gulf, which is over 1 500 kilometers long, contains one of the most spectacular and richest seas in biological terms. In this enormous ecosystem, 40% of Mexico's fishing yield is obtained, and 35% of the world's species of cetaceans is found there. A great diversity of species inhabits its waters: close to 4 000 invertebrates and over 1 000 vertebrates. To a great extent, this is due to a series of physical, chemical, and biological phenomena: the Earth's rotation, the strong tides, and the winds that come down from the mountains make its currents powerful and turbulent, mobilizing the cold waters in the deep ocean trenches. These waters, which are rich in nutrients, rise to the surface by a phenomenon called upwelling. This movement results in an enormous production of plankton, which forms part of an important food chain. Plankton is eaten by sardines, anchovies, and mackerels, which in turn are eaten by tunas, jacks, birds, dolphins, and sea lions.

On a small island on the Gulf, called Rasa, is found 95% of the world's population of two species of seabirds: the elegant tern (45 000 individuals) and Heermann's gull (300 000 individuals). The former is distributed mostly in the southern hemisphere and the latter, mainly in the northern hemisphere. But not only marine mammals and seabirds find in the waters of the Gulf of California a suitable place for breeding. Turtles, sailfishes, and marlins, as well as many other species, also return there every year from faraway regions in the Pacific Ocean.

Everything is interrelated: life on Earth depends on the sea, and life in the sea depends on the land. Now more than ever before our knowledge can be turned into the most powerful instrument for making the right decisions concerning the management and conservation of the seas.

Conscious of this and as the persons responsible for CEMEX's editorial projects, we welcome the idea of producing a book on the seas, which was proposed to us by Ernesto Amtmann, Commissioner-General of Mexico at the Lisbon World Exposition, or Expo '98, dedicated to the oceans of the world.

We hope that this book, published in three languages and distributed in various countries, will become a tool and a catalyst for awakening interest throughout the world in studying, making rational use of, and conserving our seas. Over half the copies to be printed will be donated to different conservationist organizations which will utilize them to raise funds for their projects, and as a means for creating awareness in society. Thus, *Celebration of the Seas: Heritage for the Future* can enrich us with experiences and amaze us with visions, anecdotes, challenges, and images that show us all that we can lose, the great diversity of life forms and the contrasting beauty of the species that dwell in the seas of this planet.

In the lives of those of us who have had the opportunity to come into contact with the sea, it has inspired in us different sensations, and we all feel a sense of wonder at its majesty. That is why we invited a select group of sealovers to tell us of their personal impressions and experiences, and to share with us their commitments and fears regarding the future of the oceans. Diverse opinions and activities related to the sea came together in these pages. The answer was overwhelming: it was as if the sea itself had asked them to speak on its behalf.

We received images from many photographers and brief essays from explorers, researchers, writers, and conservationists, in response to this "call from the sea." We are fortunate and proud to include contributions by the following authors in this book: Thor Heyerdahl, the legendary explorer of the world's oceans; Kathryn S. Fuller, president of the World Wildlife Fund; Bill Curtsinger and Tui De Roy, world-renowned photographers and writers; Mark Van Putten, president of the National Wildlife Federation; Michael Gore, ornithologist and photographer who has travelled the world over; Jorge Soberón, executive secretary of the Comisión Nacional para el Conocimiento y Uso de la Biodiversidad; Enriqueta Velarde, scientist and conservationist; Martha Hill, former photo editor of the *Audubon* magazine; Pablo Cervantes, biologist and photographer; Sylvia A. Earle, marine biologist and pioneer of deep diving; Christine Eckstrom, Carlos Eyles, and Michelle A. Gilders, experienced writers on nature themes; Stanton A. Waterman, one of the most outstanding directors of underwater films and documentaries in recent times; Michael Small, diplomat and promoter of the conservation of the seas of the world; and Richard Weber, explorer of the Arctic.

In view of how important the oceans have been for humankind throughout its history, and the significance they have for its future, this book is dedicated to a celebration of the seas —those waters that embrace us, that keep us together on a planet rich in biodiversity— with great respect and steadfast hope.

PATRICIO ROBLES GIL
President
Agrupación Sierra Madre

THE AGELESS OCEANS
Thor Heyerdahl

Planet Earth was a ball of fire when it started circling around the sun together with its sister planets at the birth of light and time. When the crust cooled off and big and small planets took their present solid form, this was the only one in our solar system to be blessed with an ocean. Whether we believe in the ancient scriptures or in modern science, the ocean on our blue planet is older than any continent or island. When Planet Earth took its spherical shape, no earth was seen; it was a water-covered ball racing through emptiness, glowing hot inside but with ocean water clinging to all its sides. Due to the tremendous heat, Planet Earth was totally sterile with no organic elements to generate the growth of any living species. The first miracle of the creation of substance, referred to by modern astronomers as the Big Bang, was to produce the immense power of gravity holding the entire ocean tight to all sides of the flying ball without a drop splashing off and spilling into space. Every drop of precious water was reserved and needed to set into motion the first and only true perpetuum mobile designed to create the evolution of life on Earth.

With the formation of a global ocean, the newborn planet got a heart and began pumping water up and around. Purified water evaporated and rose from the surface towards the sky to form drifting clouds. But not so high that they were lost into space. They formed an outer umbrella of humidity at a restricted distance above the ocean, holding fresh water in reserve for rain. The drifting clouds sprinkled rainwater down again everywhere, back into the same ocean that had sent it into the sky. The same water, up and down eternally. The invisible forces behind evaporation and gravity kept the water in perpetual motion and not a drop was lost into the universe. But the circulating water was still as sterile as the hardened crust of rock beneath it.

When finally land arose from the bottom of the sea and formed the first continents and islands, rain created freshwater lakes and streams that rushed through the landscape back to the sea. Seasonal temperature changes with ice, running water and winds caused erosion, and sterile particles of salts and minerals were washed downhill to create a witches' brew in the global sea. Then another miracle happened: Rays from the sun fertilized the sterile planet. Molecules in the salts and minerals combined to form the first living cells, and soon the ancestors of all plants and animals including humans were drifting helplessly around with the ocean currents.

Another invisible power created the first genes programmed for further evolution. The cells multiplied and eyes, fins and tails grew forth, permitting animal species to see and move about at will. An infinity of species evolved, from jellyfish and sea urchins to fish and whales. All that grows and moves on the surface of our planet today came out of the witches' brew that churned about as currents in the ocean. All of us who can speak and love and fight on dry land today have common ancestors who came out of the salty seas.

Our dependence on our distant relatives in the ocean has never ended. Darwin may be justified when he argues that the diversity of species evolved through the survival of the fittest, but we must never forget that even the least fit are needed to help the fittest to survive. The single-celled plankton that started evolution is just as necessary for us today as when it was miraculously born from sterile salts and minerals. It was the first single-celled plankton that started to produce oxygen at a time when only a mixture of poisonous gases surrounded the planet. This plankton was needed in enormous quantities until so much oxygen was produced that it rose above the surface of the waters and, with added help from plant species that took root ashore, created the atmosphere. Only then was it possible for marine species to develop lungs and crawl up ashore and become the ancestors of all terrestrial species. Take away the plant plankton today, and the dwindling forests will not suffice to produce the quantity of oxygen humans and animals need to continue survival.

Even as a terrestrial species, most of humankind has for millions of years returned to the sea for an endless supply of food. Archaeology can demonstrate what a marine diet has meant for survival on all the islands and continental coasts. Mollusks, shellfish, and fish were picked and caught along all shorelines tens of thousands of years before humans built the first boat and, from the moment the art of boatbuilding began, a new important step helped humans on their rapid climb to the building of culture and civilization.

Humans hoisted sail before they saddled a horse. They poled and paddled along rivers and navigated the open seas before they travelled on wheels along a road. Watercraft were the first of all vehicles. With them, the Stone Age world began to shrink. By hoisting sail or merely travelling with the current, early humans were

Brown booby in flight. Cocos Island, Costa Rica. © **Kevin Schafer** able to settle the islands. Territories that could be reached overland only by generations of gradual transmigration for those who had to confront obstacles like swamps and lifeless tundra, naked mountains and impenetrable jungles, glaciers and deserts could be reached in weeks by casual drift or by navigation. Watercraft were humans' first major tool for their conquest of the world.

All available evidence shows that it was the papyrus ship which developed all the seagoing ship's characteristic properties and which subsequently became the model for the wooden ship, not the other way round. The design of the papyrus ship was already developed when the First Dynasty began building pyramids along the Nile.

Data indicate that it was somewhere around 3000 BC that the Middle East pioneers in maritime architecture took the revolutionary step of replacing compact papyrus bundles with a hollow wooden hull, imitating —throughout a long transition period— the characteristic lines of their previous reed ships. People with access to the easily split and incredibly durable Lebanon cedar, like the Hittites and the Phoenicians, were early to abandon papyrus reeds for boatbuilding, a material they had received through overseas trade with Egypt. Next, the Egyptians themselves began importing cedar from Lebanon, building their own wooden pleasure and cargo vessels on the Nile.

No matter how perfectly they were built, reed ships could not compete with wooden vessels in durability. The rope lashings encircling the bottom would gradually chafe off if a reed vessel were beached too often, and a couple of years would probably be a fair lifetime for a major reed ship in frequent use. Undoubtedly, the superior durability and speed of the wooden ship counted more in the long run than any of the virtues of the early type of bundle boat. Yet these were not negligible; the reed boat offered far greater security at sea and a superior carrying capacity.

Thus the modern sailing ship, with its early Mediterranean ancestry, combines two pedigrees, beginning respectively with a hollow tree trunk and a bundle of floating reeds.

Before humans ventured into the ocean, rivers are known to have been their first highways through landscapes covered by thick forests that hid unknown ene-

mies and all the dangers of the original wilderness. Early settlements developed into ocean ports at the mouth of rivers. Migrations penetrating the continents of Asia, Africa, Europe, and America are known to have taken full advantage of nature's inland waterways. Founders of civilizations have been lured along the rivers Indus, Euphrates, Tigris, Nile, Volga, Danube and Magdalena, to mention just a few of the more conspicuous cases. We notice the rivers no matter how slowly and smoothly they may flow through the land. But we do not see the ocean currents, and are therefore apt to forget the greatest and mightiest of all streams; they have banks of water and flow invisibly through the sea. The largest river with its source in Peru is not the Amazon, flowing eastward through Brazil, but the Humboldt Current flowing westward through the Pacific. The mightiest river of Africa is not the Nile, but the Canary Current with its delta between the Caribbean Islands, emptying African seawater into the Mexican Gulf. The fixed itineraries of these marine rivers span the oceans and form paths between the continents.

The invisible rivers which float across all major oceans, stronger and larger than any river ashore, are held in constant motion by nothing less than the rotation of the Earth itself. They flow from east to west in the tropical belt, and striking continents they turn, each in a wide loop, coming back east in colder latitudes as near as possible to the Arctic and Antarctic regions. These tropical currents do not move alone; they pull with them any floating thing, while above the sea the eternal trade winds blow with full strength in the same general direction, from east to west, the year around. Dwarfing the continental rivers as conveyor belts, they are even more one-way directed because of the permanent company of the extremely forceful easterly trade winds. Where visible coasts and premeditated decisions have not guided humans in search of new land, the invisible marine conveyors have been ever present to lure them from one coast to the next with or without the traveller's own wish and awareness.

When it comes to ocean travel, four basic misconceptions must be cleared away before discussions on primitive seafaring possibilities become anywhere near realistic:

1. A watertight hull is not the only, nor is it the best, solution for security at sea.

Magnificent frigate bird, adult male. Galápagos Islands, Ecuador. © **Wayne Lynch**

In a vessel with a wash-through body, the building material is self-buoyant, boring worms are no threat, and bailing is superfluous since any sea breaking on board will merely run through and leave the vessel on top of the waves as before. The shallow draft and compact body structure permit such vessels to voyage among reefs and shoals and to make crash landings on coasts which no hulled vessel could approach.

2. It is wrong to believe that security in ocean travel invariably increases with the size of the vessel and the height of its deck above sea level. It is a great advantage to a vessel to be small enough to move freely between and over the swells, since a boat much over thirty feet long will either be forced to bury bow or stern into surrounding waves, or will bridge two waves simultaneously with the risk of breaking amidships.

3. The idea that it is easier and safer for primitive navigators to hug the continental coastline than to cross an open ocean is a very common illusion, contrary to the facts. Whether in storm or normal weather, nowhere are the oceans more treacherous than near coasts and over shallows. Nowhere do the seas raise steeper and more dangerous waves than where ocean rollers meet the backwash from cliffs and, as a result, increase in chaotic interference with tides and deflected currents. In mid-ocean there are no rocks or reefs to interfere with the progress of either craft or currents; the swells are drawn long and regular, and the peril of wrecking is reduced to an absolute minimum.

4. The logical conclusion that the distance from A to B equals the distance from B to A is correct ashore, but wrong at sea. For instance, the distance from Peru to the Tuamotu Islands is 4 000 miles, but after traversing only a quarter of that distance, or about 1 000 miles of ocean surface, the *Kon-Tiki* raft had already reached the Tuamotu Archipelago from Peru. The reason is, of course, that the ocean surface had displaced itself about 3 000 miles in the direction of Polynesia during the period of 101 days of the crossing. The raft had benefited from an invisible free lift from the Humboldt Current, running like a river from Peru through Polynesia. If another aboriginal type of vessel had been able to sail with straight course in the opposite direction at the very same speed, it would have had to move upstream and cross no less than 7 000 miles of running seawater to reach Peru from the Tuamotu Archi-

pelago. That is, about seven times the sailing distance and sailing time confronting the *Kon-Tiki*, although the distance would be exactly the same on a map. In addition, no sailing vessel can advance in a straight line directly into the wind, so in trying to force its way in the opposite direction to that taken by the *Kon-Tiki*, it would also have to tack against the powerful trade winds and thus add another couple of thousand miles to the straight 7 000-mile itinerary.

The ocean seems endless, except to raft voyagers and astronauts. But it merely winds around the continents like a lake, with land enclosed inside and on all sides. And it clings to the planet like the peel of an orange that also seems endless, because it begins again wherever it ends.

The ocean has lived for an estimated four billion years, to judge from bacteria and other microorganisms embedded in the oldest rocks. Throughout all those ages, the ocean has been the global filter. Untold masses of pollution from carcasses, excrement, and rotting vegetation have entered the one and only ocean, from all the rivers or with silt from all the shorelines. The number of prehistoric monsters, the whales and fish and plankton that have died and decomposed in the sea would have been enough to silt up all the water if not decomposed and recycled to new, young, smaller life. The molecules of all matter entering the sea from land and air decompose and are rebuilt, and nothing but pure water is allowed to evaporate and rise to the clouds. Thus, the clockwork has moved smoothly and in the interest of global life and sanitation for billennia, the sea sending only clean water back to the land with the clouds, and gravity sweeping all dirt downhill into the sea, where it is digested and transformed. The clockwork was built as a perpetuum mobile, and as such it would work forever with the ocean as a filter, if humans had kept their modern molecules tied up in their own laboratories.

But after one-time use, humans no longer want their everlasting molecules, nor any control as to where they all end. Most detergents and insecticides are absorbed as by blotting paper into all organic life. And once inside they can never again get out. They enter the life cycle of plants and are eaten by beasts. They follow the universal current of the life cycle, which ends up in the sea. But while all the molecules of nature are eaten by microorganisms and are digested to form new

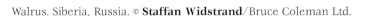

Walrus. Siberia, Russia. © **Staffan Widstrand**/Bruce Coleman Ltd.

living cells, those made by humans are indigestible, nondegradable, and enter to be stored in the living cell. Most of the hydrocarbons float and stay in the surface layer of the ocean. And that it where the plankton lives. And most of it comes from outlets along the coasts. And that is the breeding place and home of the bulk of marine life.

A constant stream of seawater runs through the body of plankton. Nature's molecules are digested. But not those composed by humans. They get stuck in the body of the plankton, and plankton is drifting everywhere to act jointly as the ocean's giant vacuum cleaner. They leave the water clean but are themselves swallowed in vast numbers by mollusks, crustaceans, and fish. Thus, the molecules made by humans accumulate in ever-stronger concentrations as they follow the food chain up to humans' cooking pots. And no matter how much we cook and how much we chew, we can never destroy the nondegradable and venomous molecules we have produced in an unfortunate attempt to improve our environment.

What the farmer and the housewives spray out of plastic bottles, the fishermen and the middlemen bring back from the ocean and serve us on our own plates.

If humankind hurts the ocean, we hurt ourselves and our descendants. If the plankton in the ocean dies, we on dry land will die from suffocation. A dead ocean means a dead planet.

IMPRESSIONS OF THE ARCTIC OCEAN AND THE NORTH POLE
Richard Weber

I am a polar explorer. I push the limits of human physical and psychological endurance on the Arctic Ocean. During the past ten years, I have spent more than 400 days travelling on the Arctic Ocean. The Arctic Ocean has been my chosen domain because it is unique in the world, it is always challenging, and it is relatively unexplored as compared to other areas.

The North Pole lies in the center of 14 million square kilometers of Arctic

Ocean, 750 kilometers from the closest land. The North Pole is the top of the world, the point where all time zones and lines of longitude meet —there is no time, just six months of daylight followed by six months of darkness. It is a mathematical as well as a mystical point. Man has been struggling to reach it for over 150 years by boat, dogsled, airplane, balloon, on foot, skis, motorcycle, snowmobile, even by horse. Yet when you get there, there is nothing to see. You cannot see the North Pole. There is no North "Pole," it is an imaginary point invented two thousand years ago by Greek astrologists. Before GPS (Global Positioning System), a visitor to the Pole could only be certain of being within the area of the North Pole with a precision of one or two nautical miles. Nothing better was available. Yet each spring, this spot still draws adventurers, visitors, and scientists.

The evidence strongly suggests that the early explorers never reached the Pole. The first people to stand at the Pole were Russian pilots who arrived by plane in 1939. In 1968 an insurance salesman from Minnesota, Ralph Plaistad, crossed the surface of the Arctic Ocean by snowmobile. At the Pole, he was evacuated by aircraft. Since the turn of the century, the equipment has improved but the ice remains the same. It is a tough and difficult journey; less than 100 people have reached the Pole compared to many hundreds who have climbed Everest. The modern trend is to journey across the ice of the Arctic Ocean "unsupported," that means, with no outside assistance, no resupplies by aircraft, no machines and at the Pole to be evacuated by aircraft. Less than 15 people have been successful at this. In the spirit of the turn-of-the-century explorers, who had no aircraft for North Pole evacuation, only two people, Weber and Malakhov, have reached the Pole and returned with no outside assistance.

The Arctic Ocean is a deceiving place. Everyone has heard of the dangers of climbing Mount Everest, high altitude, avalanches, high winds, and crevasses. Dozens of books and films have been written and produced. But there are only a handful of North Pole books and no really good, accurate documentary films. How hard can it be to cross a few hundred kilometers of flat ice? After all, modern adventurers at the other pole, in Antarctica, routinely sail up to 200 kilometers per day. A few years ago, one British postman cheerfully declared that he was going to walk across the

Pack ice. Beaufort Sea, Canadian Arctic. © **Wayne Lynch**

Arctic Ocean to the North Pole. Back home in Britain, he could walk 80 kilometers in a single day. It is 750 kilometers to the Pole, that's nine days, a few extra days for bad weather, so he planned for two weeks. On his first or second day he fell into the water and ended his polar journey.

The Arctic Ocean is not a flat surface. Much of it is covered with a permanent ice cap three to four meters thick. Like any other ocean, it is alive. It moves. All the pack ice on the Ocean is drifting. When you awake in the morning, you are not in the same place as when you camped the night before. As the ice moves, some pieces called (ice) pans push together to form pressure ridges or pull apart to leave cracks of open water. It is like a scale model of the Earth's surface, where tectonic plates push together thrusting up mountains or pull apart leaving cracks of open water. American explorer Will Steger once compared the surface of the Arctic Ocean to the layer of dust floating on a bucket of water. Perhaps it is more accurate to describe it as a layer of dust on a slow-moving river. When the "layer of dust" cracks, a traveller is confronted with open water. These cracks have to be bypassed on foot, which can take hours, or you can wait until the ice freezes. If the crack is narrow and you are feeling adventurous, you can build a bridge with ice and snow and ski across it quickly before it sinks into the water.

As a journey on the Arctic Ocean is a journey on water, it has to be attempted when the ice conditions are best. During the winter it is dark, not good for travelling. In early March the sun returns to the shores of the ocean and adventurers can set off. The temperatures are the coldest at this time of year, getting as low as −60 degrees Celsius. At this temperature skin can freeze in seconds, plastic shatters, and a match can be extinguished in gasoline. As the sun rises, so does the temperature but ice conditions deteriorate. By mid–June the ice pack is so loose that travel is impossible. The ice pack becomes a collection of loose pans floating this way and that at the whim of the weather.

The ice on the Russian side of the Arctic Ocean is young, three to five years old. It is flatter, smoother, and the pressure ridges are smaller. Over on the Canadian side, the ice pushes up against the coast, piling up year after year, getting thicker and thicker, for up to 25 years before it slips out into the Greenland Sea. The pressure ridges push up to 20 meters. Huge areas, hectare after hectare, are completely smashed. Enormous pressure ridges run throughout like mountain ranges. In amongst the ice blocks where the wind can't reach, the snow is soft and deep.

The Arctic Ocean has many moods. It can be the most amazing landscape with blue sky, brilliant sun and sparkling snow, and ice blocks of turquoise, blue, green, grey, and black. There are snowdrifts carved into wondrous shapes by the wind, and the open water is a marvelous Caribbean blue-green. A few hours later, there can be a howling blizzard, blowing snow, screaming wind, and zero visibility. Or it can be a calm whiteout with everything one white-grey color, the sky, the snow, the ice. It is hard to tell where one begins and the other ends. With no shadows and no definition, walking is agonizing. You trip over the drifts and fall into holes. I always have the impression that to walk in such conditions must be a little like being blind. On the horizon the vapor from open water rises like columns of sinister black smoke. The water is black and evil-looking. There is no wind and no sound. The only sound is your heartbeat and the squeaking of your skis.

At the Pole the ice drifts an average of five kilometers per day; on a windy day it can drift 20 to 30 kilometers. I have been in the awkward position of skiing toward the Pole at two kilometers per hour while drifting backwards at almost one kilometer per hour. The result is only one kilometer of net gain for each hour of struggle. Another time I have drifted ten kilometers in "my" direction while I slept.

The Arctic Ocean is completely unpredictable. This is why travel on its surface is so challenging. Every morning you just do not know what the day will bring: rough ice, flat ice, open water, good or bad visibility, good or bad weather, positive or negative drift. You can never tell if an expedition will be successful until it is completed, the final steps taken. Even an "easy" expedition is not a guaranteed success. In 1997, there were five independent groups on short one- to two-week expeditions skiing the final kilometers to the Pole. These were commercial trips with paying clients, but only one group, the one with the experienced guides, reached the Pole.

Even in this frozen environment there is some life. Under the ice there are a few fish, hunted by even fewer seals. On the ice, polar bears and arctic foxes wander in search of the seals. The polar bear is one of the few animals that is not afraid

Harp seal pup. Quebec, Canada. © **Norbert Rosing**

of humans. In such an environment, where humans are nonexistent, a bear may pass its entire life without ever making human contact. A wandering traveller is just a weird seal, potential food in a land where food is scarce. This does not mean that all bears are aggressive, but a traveller must always be prepared to have a curious bear wander into camp to investigate the strange smells. Bears have been known to attack and maim people on the Arctic Ocean.

It is the simplicity of travel on the Arctic Ocean that is compelling. It is a constant challenge, never the same. Out there, life is reduced to an equation of eating, sleeping, and skiing. The main concerns are the weather and ice drift. Friends and families are removed. Mortgages do not matter. Life is finely focussed on making (nautical) miles. Teamwork, perseverance, and clear thinking are all important. It is not the visit to the Pole that matters, after all the Pole is just another piece of pack ice, "here today and gone tomorrow." It is the journey to the Pole that counts, it's getting there. The Pole is a piece of drifting ice. A journey to the Pole is the experience of traversing the Arctic Ocean with all its moods. It is also a journey within yourself. Any difficult struggle changes you and a polar struggle is no different. When people overcome adversity and go beyond their individual limits, they become stronger. That's what happens on a polar journey; you plan, prepare, train, then you undertake the trip with all its hazards and hardships. You succeed, then you are stronger. If you are not successful, hopefully you have wasted only your time. After all, in the words of British explorer Robert Swan, "It is a place that wants you dead, let up your guard and it will take you."

It is so very easy to look at the Arctic and the Arctic Ocean as a huge and empty virgin expanse. But a closer look shows that humans, through clumsiness, neglect, ignorance, and stupidity have made a "good" start at destroying this wonderful and ecologically fragile place.

The central Arctic Ocean is an indicator of the health of the world. When compared to the other oceans on Earth, it is relatively small. The water flows in through the Bering Strait and out the other side into the Greenland Sea. The ocean in the middle is over four kilometers deep. Pollutants are deposited as the water moves through these deep areas. Though very few people and virtually no industry line the shores of the Arctic Ocean, the large mammals such as seals, whales, and walruses are polluted with PCBs and other chemicals. Animals that have perhaps never encountered a human being are carrying human waste, simply because they happen to be at the top of the food chain.

In the 1950s Arctic haze first appeared. These airborne pollutants are carried in the air from Europe, Russia, and other places, over the Arctic Ocean and deposited with the snow or rain. Industrial pollution, even radioactive pollution, can be measured in the snow that lies on the surface of the Arctic Ocean. Even at the North Pole, thousands of kilometers from civilization, a clear horizon is a rare event. Normally, on a clear day the horizon is a dirty yellow, like the brownish yellow smog that lies over a big city. To the traveller who has flown thousands of kilometers by small aircraft for many hours or skied for several months, it is a rude reminder that no portion of our world, no matter how remote, is immune from the ravages of humankind when it starts polluting.

In isolated places on the shores of the Arctic Ocean, the military machines of the Cold War have also taken their toll on the environment. In Russian Siberia, certain areas are dotted with nuclear dumps and industrial pollution. In northern Canada, the DEW Line Defense System built by the American military stretches across the Arctic. Now mostly abandoned, the sites continue to leak pollutants such as PCBs and fossil fuels. In Canada, where more money is available (than in Russia) and public pressure is stronger, some cleanups have started.

IF I WERE A SEAL...
Bill Curtsinger

Diving has long been considered a quiet endeavor. When I was a young boy, I read Cousteau's book *The Silent World* several times, and thought then that the world beneath the waves was a pretty quiet place. Nothing could be farther from the truth. The sea is a cacophony of noise. Sound travels faster and further underwater than

Green sea turtle. Michoacán, Mexico. © **Bill Curtsinger**

it does in air. If you pause in your breathing cycle underwater to let your bubbles surface, you can hear all sorts of strange and wonderful sounds. Beneath the annual sea ice of McMurdo Sound, Antarctica, you can hear a snow tractor crunching across the sea ice above. You can hear trucks go by. You can hear the rumble of an aircraft landing on the ice at Williams Field, an airport on the sea ice two miles away. You can hear Weddell seals.

Weddell seals are, for me, the aboriginals of the Antarctic, the natives, the locals, the year-rounders. They don't go north to the pack ice for the winter, or to the relative warmth of some subantarctic island. With the world above freezing over, and other species heading north, while the Antarctic descends into the darkness of another polar winter, Weddell seals are happily going about their business under the ice.

They distinguish themselves from other Antarctic species in many ways, one is by being the southernmost naturally occurring mammal in the world. They also happen to be one of the deepest diving mammals on Earth. They have recorded for science a dive to about 600 m for over an hour. Take it from me, that is quite a feat for a fellow mammal. They have very large eyes adapted to low light levels beneath the ice. They maintain breathing holes with their teeth. And if that weren't enough, they possess a complicated sonar system to catch prey and navigate their way back to their breathing hole. And they produce a bizarre and wonderful song I can only describe as an otherworldly trill. You can hear that song underwater.

Imagine yourself, for a moment, a Weddell seal. Look up at the ceiling in the room where you now sit. Imagine it the underside of the ice and the ceiling of your world, with only one tiny hole from which you can breathe. You are 600 m beneath that ceiling of ice and a long way laterally from the little hole that happens to be the only access you have to the sweet air above. It is dark. You have just spent the better part of an hour hunting for a giant Antarctic cod. A little internal bell starts to ring in your lungs, time to go up. You will trill your way calmly back to that breathing hole, maybe with a fish, maybe not. There are hundreds, thousands of Weddell seals doing just that right now. May the trilling go on.

I was walking along an Antarctic beach once, and came across an animal's

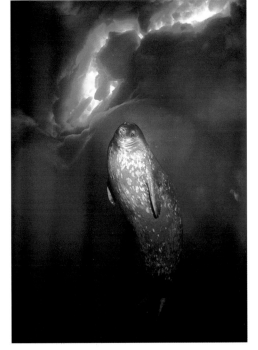

skull. It had washed ashore in a storm. The skull had been tossed around some, but there were a few teeth still left in the upper jawbone. The skull was obviously from a seal, but the teeth were very un-seallike. The teeth have several rounded points that look like little enameled waves frozen at their crest. These teeth are not from a seal that bites into and eats a lot of flesh. The upper and lower rows of teeth interlock to form a kind of strainer. The teeth are from what is, for some unexplained reason, commonly called a crabeater seal (*Lobodon carcinophagus*). They do not eat crabs, they eat mostly krill, the euphausid shrimplike crustacean, the primary member of the food chain in the southern ocean. They eat lots of krill, some 60 million tons by some estimates, and their un-seallike teeth are designed with this food source in mind. Gulping whole mouthfuls of swarming krill, the crabeater uses its teeth as a strainer, and just pushes out the water and swallows its meal.

Crabeaters are *the* seal of the great Antarctic pack ice. Pack ice is drifting pieces of seasonal sea ice broken up by wind and wave action. The pack ice is circumpolar and its journey is at the mercy of oceanic circulation. This is real crabeater country, where they feed, mate, give birth on the ice platform, and tend to their young. The pack ice has to be near shore or else one goes by boat to it to see crabeater seals. Only rarely have they ever been seen ashore.

The Antarctic pack ice is home to other marine mammals, among them leopard seals and killer whales. Killer whales hunt in packs that seem to be made up of their big extended family. They are very impressive hunters. In the world of marine mammals, there is not much doubt as to their superior "intelligence." They like to eat crabeater seals. I have seen killer whales tip over an iceberg to dump a small group of crabeater seals into the sea. I have heard another story that I did not witness myself, but based on my own observations and the people who related the story separately, I very much believe it.

There was a large pack of killer whales spy-hopping around a very large piece of frozen pack ice, about one hundred meters square. The ice was too large to tip over. The whales swam away and the observers, who were on board an Antarctic research vessel, thought they were gone. A minute later they saw a line of killer whales swimming rapidly towards the ice floe. They were creating a wave of sea water. They submerged at the edge of the ice, with their wave cresting up onto the floe and washing off several crabeater seals. A few seals managed to scramble back onto the floe. Some did not. The water around and beneath the ice floe was red. I believe every word of this story.

Crabeater young are also attacked by the only predatory seal in the world, the leopard seal. Many crabeaters are scarred with old symmetrical stripes along their flanks, obvious teeth marks from an early lesson in life about survival on the pack ice.

I often wonder how the seal whose skull I was holding met its fate; killer whale, leopard seal, disease, old age? I have picked up and pondered hundreds, if not thousands of items from beaches around the world. Like the seal skull, certain found objects generate thoughts and feelings that will be with you forever. Whenever I beachcomb, I try and keep the following in mind: For every object I pick up there could be a hundred questions, and not many answers.

My introduction to the law of the jungle came, of all places, on a distant ice-covered beach at Cape Crozier in the Antarctic. It was here, at Cape Crozier, where I began to develop an understanding and appreciation for the animal world. The minutiae of my college biology course suddenly seemed, well, relevant. Old terms challenged my intellectual curiosity anew: evolution, ecology, ethology, survival strategies, reproductive biology, predator-prey relationships. Cape Crozier was where the pieces of the larger puzzle of the animal world started to fit together. Working on this puzzle has been a lifelong quest for me. The puzzle will never be finished, of course, but the journey is an exciting one. It was also here at Cape Crozier that I first realized I wanted to be a seal. I wanted to really see them, swim in their world, think like a seal, and try to place myself somewhere along the path of their daily lives in order to learn something new and bring their secretive world to the printed page. Weeks of watching leopard seals from the ice front at Cape Crozier did this to me. My life has not been the same since.

Of the five Phocid seals found in the Antarctic, the leopard seal is the only one that eats warm-blooded prey. A substantial portion of its diet is comprised of other seals and penguins. Leopard seals have a fondness for eating the juveniles of every pinniped found in the southern ocean. They also eat emperor, chinstrap, king, gentoo, crested, Magellanic, and especially Adélie penguins.

Adélie penguins are the most abundant and widely distributed penguin in the Antarctic. The Adélie penguin rookery at Cape Crozier numbers some 300 000 birds, and leopard seals capture them as they swim to and from their nest sites onshore.

THE LARGEST "HOME" FOR LIFE
Kathryn S. Fuller

Most people do not appreciate how critical the oceans are to life on Earth. Covering two thirds of the Earth's surface, oceans feature prominently in global physical, chemical, and biological processes and provide the largest "home" for life on this planet. Oceans absorb three million tons of carbon dioxide a year, provide lifesaving medicines and the world's single largest source of animal protein, and sustain a variety of species —from jawless fish to giant squids, from microscopic phytoplankton to mammoth blue whales. The complexity of life in the sea is in fact greater than on land.

But our irreplaceable oceans are now in jeopardy. The combined stresses of overfishing, coastal development, pollution, and illegal trade in endangered species have imperiled oceans and the plant and animal life they sustain.

The numbers are telling:

- Ten percent of the world's coral reefs have vanished and another 60 percent are at risk.
- Nearly half the planet's salt marshes and mangrove forests have been drained and cleared.
- Many of the world's fisheries are overfished and at risk of destruction.
- Populations of important large oceanic predators —tunas, swordfish, marlins, and sharks— have declined by more than 80 percent in the last two decades.

On top of that, destructive fishing practices are driving such endangered species as Steller's sea lions to the brink of extinction; land-based pollution is trig-

Face of scorpion fish. Red Sea. © **Burt Jones**/**Maurine Shimlock**/Secret Sea

gering fish kills and massive algal blooms; and synthetic chemicals are undermining wildlife's ability to survive and reproduce.

With time running out for our oceans and the rich variety of life they house, a concerted global effort is needed to save them.

My own stake in the ocean realm goes back to graduate studies in marine ecology. My first experiences of the undersea world were nothing less than a revelation. The richness, beauty, and complexity of what I saw was truly marvelous —from tiny crustaceans buried in sand mounds to the intricate dynamics of coral reef communities of vertebrates and invertebrates. Thanks to that initial exposure, conservation of the marine environment took on a new, very personal and important meaning for me.

My commitment to marine conservation is one shared by many others around the world. Our efforts are complicated, though, by the fact that much of what we are trying to save is out of sight. Oceans may be in some respects more threatened than our lands, but the average citizen continues to view the world through a terrestrial lens.

For that reason, many people who are deeply informed about, say, deforestation, may know comparatively little about the crises facing our marine environments. How many people know that during the late 1970s and 1980s, nearly 80 percent of the grasses in America's Chesapeake Bay disappeared —taking with them critical habitat for a host of fish, crabs, and other species? Had 80 percent of the forests of Appalachia disappeared during that period, it would surely have provoked a massive outcry. Here, it went largely unnoticed.

World Wildlife Fund is working to sound the alarm. Through our Global Marine Initiative we are seeking to raise awareness and concern in order to protect not just marine species but also the biological processes that have animated our oceans for

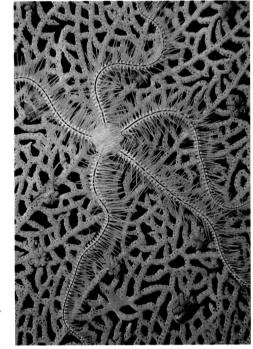

billions of years. This initiative is part of WWF's ongoing Living Planet Campaign, dedicated to conserving the world's most biologically important terrestrial, freshwater, and marine habitats. WWF scientists have used computerized mapping technology to identify roughly 200 of the world's most outstanding ecoregions, and of these, 61 are marine environments —from the mangroves of East Africa to the Philippines' Sulu Sea, from Australia's Great Barrier Reef to the legendary Galápagos Islands.

Drawing on this comprehensive framework, WWF is now pioneering new approaches that attempt to apply conservation principles across entire ecoregions. Our first generation of pilot projects will target such areas as the Bering Sea ecoregion —one of the world's most productive marine ecosystems, with some 450 species of fish, crustaceans, and mollusks, 50 species of seabirds, and 25 species of mammals. We hope that management techniques developed here will create new models for conserving marine resources on larger, more biologically meaningful scales.

Conservation investments like these can reap large dividends, both in resource protection and in the advancement of knowledge. Consider this: In the last few years alone, scientists have discovered whole new groups of organisms living in deep-sea vents, flourishing independent of sunlight and resembling no other life form ever encountered. Who knows what other mysteries are waiting to be unlocked in our oceans' depths? Who knows what medicinal, biological, or economic treasures are waiting to be tapped?

That is why educating the public about the threats to our marine systems is so critical. If a book like this can show us how much we stand to lose and enrich our understanding of the challenges we face in protecting and restoring our oceans for the future, it will have accomplished its mission.

Brittle star and basket star on gorgonian. Florida, USA. © **Mike Bacon**

THE OTHER THREE QUARTERS
Pablo Cervantes

What I have searched for in the oceans is true knowledge about humankind and myself. I now know that those of us who allow ourselves to be enveloped by the sea will never again be full-time landsmen, and that the mere contemplation of its peaceful surface instills in us understanding, love, and inner peace, which lead us to something simply called integrity.

RAMÓN BRAVO

Another day in our research cruise on the Gulf of California had come to an end. Aboard the cutter that was taking us through the waters surrounding the islands, we calmly rocked back and forth cutting through the waves under a setting sun. We had no idea of what was in store for us.

Looking toward the horizon, suddenly we saw something we could not quite describe, but which was definitely not a common sight. We immediately steered the cutter toward what was so powerfully attracting our attention. Soon thereafter, the sea seemed to be boiling and the sky turned dark intermittently. A feverish activity was unfolding before our astonished eyes: thousands of dolphins were advancing rapidly to catch some of the millions of fish that were swimming this way and that in a crazed attempt to escape; veritable clouds of seabirds swooped down from the heights, diving like arrows into the water, only to emerge quickly with a fish in their beaks, then rise again and plunge once more into the water looking for prey to feed their always hungry chicks.

In just seconds we went from mere observation to a helter-skelter dash preparing cameras and diving equipment in order to experience close up what was happening. We lowered the skiff and all of a sudden found ourselves amidst a confusion of dolphins, birds, and fish that is practically impossible to describe with words. As far as the eye could see, the ocean appeared before us as we had never seen it before.

We dove into the water quickly so as to take advantage of the last rays of sunlight. Even now, some time after that day, I cannot but feel excitement when I recall that afternoon. Although I was submerged in the blue sea and there was very little light, I could distinguish before me, like phantasmagoric shadows, the swift silhouettes of the dolphins, barely perceptible among the desperate fish trying to escape.

Besides that sight, I was also captivated by the equally impressive "auditory spectacle" of those thousands of cetaceans using their sonar to locate their elusive prey. The sounds reached me from all directions. In my body I could sense the vibrations produced by this burst of life. And although we could barely see, it seemed to me that the sea was shining and that the entire universe was flowing before me.

I never knew how long I was under. At times, regardless of how quickly the events around me were occurring, I had the impression that everything was taking place in slow motion. When we surfaced, there was even more awaiting us, if that were possible: a few yards over our heads countless birds were flying here and there, disappearing from our sight before the imminent arrival of nighttime. Their splashing could be heard nearby; and although we no longer saw them swoop down, there was no doubt that their feast continued.

We returned to the skiff. The lights of the cutter were barely distinguishable in the distance, and although we were immensely elated, we hugged one another frantically and thanked Poseidon for having allowed us to enter his domain in this way; suddenly we all remained quiet, trying to assimilate what we had just witnessed. We felt the pulse of the ocean firsthand, in all its splendor; I realized, intensely, that I had not erred in my path, and that my life would continue to be joined to the sea until the end of my days.

As many city children, living far from the ocean, my first contacts with it were through books and television programs. When I was still very small, my imagination transported me to unexpected situations and places when I saw or heard anything related to the sea and its inhabitants. So I grew up with the ocean journeys of Thor Heyerdahl and his crew on primitive rafts, the travels of Jacques and Philippe Cousteau aboard the *Calypso*, the fantasy-filled adventures of "Sea Hunt," and Ramón Bravo's book and documentaries.

Several years have elapsed since then. I became a scuba diver, biologist, and nature photographer. My understanding of the oceans has been enriched thanks to my teachers and friends, but above all through my personal experiences. Remaining for months on an island, sharing daily life with its inhabitants, and learning from the simplicity and congeniality of the fishermen, swimming next to a blue whale, submerging among hundreds of hammerhead sharks or gliding over the frozen waters of the Arctic Ocean on skis are chapters of my life that have shaped my way of seeing the world and will always be with me.

Although there are yet many oceans for me to travel, I have seen enough to comprehend, for a long time now, that we have jeopardized the oceans without even

Common dolphins. Gulf of California, Mexico. © **Pablo Cervantes**/Sierra Madre

stopping to consider the consequences, some of which we are already confronting, while others could be just around the corner. For every species that dies, a world is extinguished. What has happened? Where did the days go when the waves of the sea could sing, the trees in the forests could talk, and human beings could listen and understand?

Comparing the number of years we have been *Homo sapiens* on this Earth with the time that other species have existed, it is easy to see that our presence is recent indeed. Even before the first insects flew, before most plants inhabited the Earth or dinosaurs ruled the world, sharks were already swimming in primitive oceans. They have been around for approximately 400 million years, perfectly adapted to their environment, undergoing no major changes for a long time and without altering the harmony of their habitat. We humans, in contrast, have only been on this planet for some 100 000 years. Sharks have a 399 900 000-year advantage over us, and nevertheless we have already left deep impressions on the planet, like wounds that have been unable to heal. The most serious aspect of humans' intervention is that the continuation of many species no longer depends on their own ability to survive and adapt because now nature is not the only one guiding their fate.

An optimist by instinct, I know that these same humans have crossed oceans, scaled mountains, and written music and poetry, in awe of the wonders of nature. In an era when the world was witnessing ominous times, Albert Einstein said that our technology had surpassed our humanity. Nowadays we can invert that and ensure that, as in various primitive cultures, human beings can live, as adults, seeing things through the eyes of a child. Science and technology, art and tradition. If only we could bring them together into a whole!

In a photograph sent by the *Voyager 1* spacecraft, taken beyond the orbits of Neptune and Pluto, it is possible to distinguish, with some difficulty, a small, hazy dot like millions of others in the universe. I have always said that every photograph has a heart, but in this one there are many. Once we know what this dot is, it takes on a very special meaning for all of us. It is the Earth, our Earth, where all that we know and the things for which we still lack answers have occurred or at least have originated.

From so far away it could seem that not much is happening on that little planet.

As we approach it, more and more features of its surface become visible: continents, ice masses and, above all, the blue sea that dominates all the rest. A great deal has been said about why we have named "Earth" a planet which is three quarters water, and about the fact that, although it is called "The Blue Planet," its name should be "Ocean" or "Sea." Maybe that is because, while it is true that those who named it also lived on terra firma, they lacked our fondness for the sea, but in fact, what matters is not its name but how we live on it.

On Earth, seen from outer space, it is not possible to distinguish borders dividing countries. We all share the same space, covered by the same sky and receiving light from the same sun. This planet is sea and land, jungle and desert, forest and reef, all together and coexisting. Each ecosystem is an active part of nature seen as a whole, and whatever happens to any of them, be it good or bad, has a profound effect on all the others.

Throughout the history of the world, oceans have always been closely linked to human beings' lives. If we review humankind's first testimonies, we find that in almost all mythologies, water is the foremost element. None of them goes beyond the time when the first ocean reached the borderless abyss during the eternal night, before the rest of the world was created. According to the Greeks and the Aztecs, even the gods sprang forth from the water.

We navigated in their waters before riding horses or traveling on wheels. The first vehicles were primitive rafts. We now know that humans used them consistently in Egypt over 7 000 years ago. For some countries, the sea was a very important factor in the expansion of their territorial possessions. Thanks to the sea, others found better places to live in, and to still others, the sea simply provided them with a way of quenching their thirst for delving into the unknown.

We have made it to the Moon and continue to expand our travels through space voyages when we still do not know or understand many of the mysteries held in the depths of the sea. The greatest treasures lie hidden, and the most important events take place in secrecy. We do not have to leave the Earth to see wonderful things. There are other worlds, but many of them are in this one. The lens of my camera

Ctenophore. McMurdo Sound, Antarctica. © **Bill Curtsinger**

has often become much more than that: a multicolored kaleidoscope through which both the fantastic and the unexpected pass.

Fortunately, there is still much that we can do. Striking a balance in all our actions so that the sea can continue to offer us its resources is essential. If we become protagonists in all that is happening around us and stop being mere spectators, we can be sure that there are marvelous things awaiting us. It is not true that on the verge of the twenty-first century there is nothing left to explore and discover. The so-called last frontier, the oceans, have a great deal to show us, just as we have much to learn so that the song of the whale and the flight of the albatross never cease, and the sea may maintain the equilibrium that took so long to achieve, before we humans started to submerge in it.

TO SEA AT NIGHT
Sylvia A. Earle

There is a special allure to diving at night, a shivery mix of curiosity and apprehension, the desire to explore balanced against the uncertainty of who or what might appear out of the darkness as an unwelcome surprise. For me, cool logic usually smooths the raised hairs on the back of my neck, just as it did the night I set out to explore the Coronado Escarpment, a ridged slope that plunges into deep water twelve miles offshore from San Diego, California. I sat, warm and dry, inside the clear sphere of a one-person submersible, *Deep Rover*, waiting for word from the sub's support ship that it was okay to begin my descent.

While I was still bobbing at the surface, the dark water sparkled with the cold fire of small, luminous creatures —living "stars" that merged with stars in the sky above, a surreal image of sea and space, of water, living chemistry, and unknown galaxies far away. *Is there life out there?*, I wondered. At the moment, I was surrounded by an ocean filled with a cross section of life on Earth, from microbes that reflect the earliest, deepest roots of life through more than 30 major divisions of animals and a dozen categories of plants, a living liquid flowing among billions of individual sponges, jellies, worms, mollusks, fish, mammals —and much, much more. Ninety-seven per cent of Earth's biosphere lies under the surface of the ocean.

Without water, life could not exist here or anywhere else, but water is fairly common in our solar system and in places beyond.

What about that reddish glint high in the sky — Mars?, I mused. Frozen patches of water are there, remants of once abundant rivers, streams and perhaps, a vast ocean. But was there, or is there still life thriving there? And what about another bright spot in the sky, Jupiter, and its curious moon, Europa? Tiny Europa appears to have abundant water, perhaps covered by ice, but there is no indication of life, nor of anything comparable to a blanket of air such as the life-supporting vapor engulfing Earth.

In a submersible, I am keenly aware of the air I breathe, something I tend to take for granted most of the time —until the supply is limited by the confines of my diving system, or when I remember that there is no place in the universe with a congenial atmosphere such as ours. Then I wonder anew at how special Earth is. *No other place has a life-filled ocean generating oxygen, absorbing carbon dioxide, stabilizing temperature, governing climate, weather, and overall planetary chemistry.*

"You are clear to dive!" The message stirs me to action, and I reach overhead to flood ballast tanks and begin my descent. I hope to find dense aggregations of glowing fish, clouds of jellies, squid, crustaceans, and other small creatures that in some areas tend to concentrate midwater a thousand feet or so beneath the surface. Deeper by day, closer to the surface at night, these ancient, moving communities are vital links in the ocean's transport of energy and harbor an untapped treasury of genetic wealth and scientific knowledge. Known mostly from samples taken by nets dragged from surface ships, these largely unexplored living systems are now being targeted by several nations as a source of raw materials for protein concentrate —"fish meal" for livestock food and fertilizer. "Exploit first, explore later" is a common but troubling approach.

While I was viewing the action below, others were in a small boat on the surface, sampling the same region using nets —a technique used by seagoing scientists for ages. We wanted to make some comparisons. What could I learn by *being* there that the observers on the surface could not?

I tried to imagine what aliens would know of my backyard or of any forest or city if they were high in the sky, blindly dragging nets through streets, scooping up

Jellyfish. McMurdo Sound, Antarctica. © **Bill Curtsinger**

pedestrians and chunks of buildings, a few trees and perhaps a bicycle or bus? What would they know of the way we live, the things we do —our music, or games or things we care about— if they peered into a net filled with a tangled collection of whatever happened to get snared?

As I reached 1 000 feet, a voice from above crackled over the intercom. "Sylvia! We have visitors! The sea is alive with dolphins! Spinners! Hundreds of them. Can you see them?"

I leaned into the darkness, hoping for a glimpse of a dolphin's smiling face. With lights out, it was like falling through a galaxy of glistening lantern fish, pulsing salps, sprays of brilliant blue from luminous jellyfish. I flicked the sub's lights on and a halo of small creatures became visible —small shrimp moving majestically, trailing slender antennae three times their body length; a silver-and-red speckled octopus clinging on the sub's clear surface; a plum-purple jellyfish edged with glittering threads.

Still, no dolphins. But suddenly, I could hear them! The audible rhythm of a dancing city with fluid boundaries filled the sea, its moving symphonic edge marked with soft chirps, wheeps, and staccato probing.

As their voices faded, I continued my descent, occasionally turning on the outside lights to identify creatures first glimpsed as blue flashes. More than 2 000 feet down, the concentration of small fish and minute crustaceans increased, and I hovered among them as a transparent planktonic being of sorts —but much larger than anything encountered so far.

Many times before I had examined the gelatinous goo retrieved by mid-water trawls, a slippery, diaphanous soup of crushed jellyfish, wriggling fish, silver or black, bright red shrimp, and sometimes small squids, with enormous bluish eyes hauntingly like ours. I tried to imagine what they did when they were in their element, and sometimes wondered what it might be like to *be* a squid, jetting through a dark sea, richly pigmented skin cells flashing rainbow messages to others. Or to be a jellyfish, lazily ballooning around the ocean at the whim of deep sea currents. Or a sleek cat shark, able to see the slightest flicker of blue-green from a passing fish or know of their presence using chemical or electrical field sensors that terrestrial primates can only wistfully dream about.

Now my own senses were focussed on discovering how such creatures live and what they do. A single red squid, twice as long as my hand, paused and stared at the strange mechanical monster passing through its realm. I stared back, wondering what signals must be firing in the squid's molluskan mind. The reaction of most people when encountering something unfamiliar in the sea is often, "I wonder if it's good to eat?" Or, sometimes, "I wonder if it is going to eat *me*?" The squid, however, appeared neither perturbed nor aggressive —merely curious. I had come to this place in the deep sea expecting to watch the wildlife there; it was disconcerting to find *them* watching *me*.

I continued to travel downward, finally touching bottom amid clusters of white and yellow sponges and a scattering of stalked sea feathers —soft-bodied relatives of coral and sea anemones. A bright red rockfish moved away from the light just as I noticed something puzzling in the gray-brown mud ahead —something reddish that seemed to flash in the sub's light. I eased forward to get a better look. Some deep-sea fish avoid bright light and swim away as soon as they are illuminated, others freeze, like deer mesmerized by a spotlight. This whatever-it-was stayed still, and I cautiously moved closer. I pushed gently on the manipulator control, activating the large mechanical right arm of the sub. Just before contact, I recognized the motionless red, sparkling object on its bed of silt. A soda can. *RC Cola.*

I was not really surprised. Even in the deepest, most remote reaches of the wild ocean, debris by human activity rains from above, a curiously callous kind of contact between our societies and ancient systems that until recently, have been oblivious to our existence. Most of us, meanwhile, are oblivious to theirs.

My encounter with the cola can was a jarring reminder of the many ways we are altering the sea. Since the turn of the last century, our species has added to the ocean *billions of tons* of hard trash and noxious substances that together have created unprecedented hard times for many species. Plastic debris entangles birds, fish, turtles, whales, even coral and sponges. Excess fertilizers and pesticides flowing into groundwater, streams, and rivers ultimately contaminate distant seas. Fallout from polluted skies adds stress to the waters of the world, and bit by bit, individuals are

Yellowfin tunas. Ensenada, Baja California, Mexico. © **Richard Herrmann**

affected, and systems are nudged and changed in small ways that ultimately yield big trouble.

Adding to changes brought about by what we put *in* the sea are those caused by what we take *out*. Since the early part of this century, hundreds of ocean species have been reduced to a fraction of their former abundance as a consequence of our growing appetite for them as food, fertilizer, and raw materials for various products. Some, including Atlantic cod, bluefin tuna, and swordfish, all beloved by seafood aficionados everywhere, have precipitously declined in the past twenty years, along with dozens of others whose fate depends on decisions we will make in the very near future.

From my perch in the depths, it is hard not to worry about such things, to wonder what the ocean will be like in another century. I sometimes wish I could turn my small submersible into a time machine, to dive-travel back over the ages and see coral reefs as they were when my grandparents were young, and sweep through oceans filled with haddock, cod and herring before factory trawlers found them, or visit meadows of sea grasses when they served as grazing grounds for tens of thousands of turtles, now nearly gone.

Given a chance, I couldn't resist gliding forward into the future, to meet our descendants and hear what they have to say about those of us who are around now. Will they rage at us for leaving them a planet in tatters, deprived of its resiliency? Or will they be grateful for the actions now underway to protect what we can of the living assets so vital to our survival and well-being?

As I once again adjust ballast, this time to return to the surface, I am encouraged by thoughts of a year on the verge of a new century and a new millennium when people will focus on the significance of the ocean. This is a pivotal time, perhaps a new opportunity to learn how to use, but not use up that ancient sea of plenty that sets Earth apart from Mars, from Jupiter, from all other places in all of the heavens above.

Below, meanwhile, in luminous spendor, a red squid may still be wondering what it was that intruded for a moment in a realm that was already ancient before the first dinosaur, bird or mammal ever appeared.

THE EVERCHANGING SEA
Tui De Roy

For much of my life I have crisscrossed the world's oceans in my quest to visit some of the most remote islands, from the Arctic to the Antarctic. Feelings of great anticipation always accompanied the spanning of those many blank areas on the maps —the vast seas that buffer distant lands from the rest of the familiar world—, while my thoughts were firmly fixed on what lay beyond.

But then something in me changed as I became increasingly aware of the myriad creatures for whom the world is nothing but a watery planet strewn with a few specks of irrelevant landmasses. Thousands upon thousands of the most mysterious species on Earth indeed live in or on the sea, carving out their respective niches in a web of life in comparison with which the most complex terrestrial ecosystem pales.

Yet the sea is far from uniform. Between Norway and Spitsbergen I have marveled at the sheer power of the Barents Sea unleashing foamy crests that collide in swirling fog. I have breathed the sublime purity of Drake Passage winds that rage unimpeded around the bottom of the globe, funneled between Cape Horn and the Antarctic Peninsula. I have sailed over the velvet smooth surface of the eastern tropical Pacific, where doldrum rainshowers are reflected like pools of ink on a mirror sea. Near the western edge of the same Pacific Ocean, I have teetered on angry wave crests where the Java Sea spills tumultuously into the Indian Ocean through the sieve-like chain of Indonesian islands. And where the great oceans of the world converge along the icy skirts of the frozen Antarctic continent, I have watched enthralled as the liquid world of crashing waves is metamorphosed into one of solid sea ice and icebergs, where the midnight sun plays in pastel hues of turquoise blue, salmon pink, and lavender mauve.

As my perception of the ocean realm has grown, so my attention has been drawn to the embrace of the sea like an irresistible magnet. No longer are my ocean voyages perceived as mere passages, necessary to reach the far shore, but instead have turned into journeys where the sea itself becomes the destination. And with fa-

Squids. Catalina Island, California, USA. © **Jeff Foott**

miliarity comes intimacy. What may have once appeared as a vast and monotonous watery expanse soon was revealed as an intricate mosaic of everchanging features, details, and dynamics. No two stretches of ocean are the same. Nor do two waves even resemble each other in size, angle, pitch, speed or color. Mile by mile, the salinity changes, a pocket of clear sweet water here, where little but flying fish may be found, a swirl of plankton-rich upwelling there. Currents and winds conspire to mix cool waters with warm, to drive surface layers into the abyss or draw frigid, nutrient-laden reserves back to the surface. Major streams flow from the tropics to the polar regions and back again, like never-ending, interwoven, invisible liquid ribbons entwining the Earth.

The sea's infinite though subtle variations sketch the patterns of migrations of many of its inhabitants. Gray whales swim 4 000 miles between Arctic feeding grounds and warm calving lagoons. Arctic terns fly between northern and southern polar ice in pursuit of endless summer, while wandering albatrosses may circle the globe round and round the southern ocean, their senses attuned to the subtle smells, changes of temperature, or busy sounds of undersea life that herald feeding opportunities.

My own wanderings have been sprinkled with brief encounters with these denizens of the high seas, ethereal moments sharing a few of the secrets of their daily lives before they vanish back into their own world. From the cluttered decks of a freighter, I have watched the reeling flights of petrels dancing over stormy southern seas. It is a life of perpetual motion, riding wispy airstreams over tumbling crests. The most delicate of feather adjustments, dipping a wingtip here, fanning a tail there, enable them to use the wind-speed differentials to their own advantage, harnessing the very power of wind and waves to carry them effortlessly on their lifelong errands through the raging latitudes known to sailors as the roaring forties, furious fifties, and screaming sixties.

Further south the sea loses power as it falls within the grip of the frozen pole, vast stretches of ocean held in suspended animation by perpetual ice. Walking on the fast ice that clings tenaciously to the shores of the Antarctic continent, I find it difficult to comprehend that I am truly walking over the ocean itself, miles of dark briny water spread beneath a thin frozen crust underfoot. Gigantic tabular icebergs, their ocean drift interrupted by the winter freeze, lay trapped in the sea ice like huge crystal tablelands, their glittering faces streaked with the bloodred rays of distant, slanting sun. From beneath their feet, gurgling through ice fissures and echoing up the towering faces, drift the otherworldly trills and whistles of singing Weddell seals, courting in the unseen watery world that is theirs. Across the smooth hard surface between icebergs, long snaking lines of emperor penguins glide in from far away to provision their huddled chicks. They are the only bird in the world that need never set foot on land, nesting in this seemingly sterile wonderland of frozen sea instead.

These are but a few glimpses from the most memorable of my many forays into Antarctic seas: A two-month-long circumnavigation of the entire continent by icebreaker, hugging its ice-clad shores, crunching, graunching, ramming through 12 000 miles of ocean more akin to marble than water, past a thousand icebergs carved in cathedral arches and indigo tunnels, where snow petrels fly and orcas hunt in tide cracks.

Under equatorial skies it is a very different scene that graces the eye of the ocean traveler. The line between water and air tends to be far simpler, more peaceful here than in high latitudes, often a mere quiet reflective interface between two mediums. Oxygen is not so forcefully whipped into the sea where it is calm, nor do the warmer, less saline surface layers hold the dissolved gas needed to nurture life in profusion. Tropical seas are often clear, their great creatures —giant squid, mythical oarfish, lantern fish, and a million more— secreted away in their cool depths. At the surface, flying fish evade pursuing dorados only to be snatched on the wing by plummeting red-footed boobies or fleet-winged frigate birds. Here I have drifted through the night on a becalmed sailboat under brilliant stars, listening to the explosive blow of whales filling the still air. Or by day have clung to a rope beneath the bowsprit, sharing the joys of bow-riding with a group of playful dolphins. Nearer to shore I have joined friendly, rambunctious sea lion pups bodysurfing where great ocean swells meet the shallows.

Each of these experiences has proven as blatantly different from one another as the planets in our solar system. The most extraordinary moments of my life consist of rare but magical encounters with some of the greatest animals of the deep-

Decorator crab on whip coral. Indonesia. © **Mike Severns**

est, wildest ocean, on their own terms, beneath the waves: A swim far out of sight of land with a group of sperm whales, watching the dancing rays of sunlight sink into blue-black depth, feeling the impact of their sonar clicks on my chest, then suddenly their huge, muscular shapes glide past, eyeing me in mutual curiosity before disappearing from whence they came. Closer to land, an orca feeds on a stingray while a second one follows me closely as I skin dive to watch the prey dragged gingerly by the tip of the tail out of its hiding place under a boulder. Along a deep, current-scoured wall, hammerhead sharks in formation school in their hundreds, joining green turtles at a cleaning station where smaller fish pluck away their skin parasites. Mysterious and enormous, a whale shark soars past, festooned with free-riding remoras. A fin whale, sleek like polished ebony, breaks the surface to breathe and leaves me to stare into darkness, shivering in the frigid upwelling wake thrust up by her monstrous flukes as she vanishes back into the deep. On the horizon, a sudden feeding frenzy reveals a congregation of oceanic sharks, dolphins, tuna, sea lions and diving boobies, their sinuous bodies darting together in an electrically charged melee where my vulnerability suddenly feels acute. Like an old album filled with precious snapshots, my mind is replete with oceanic memories which are as vivid as the experiences were brief.

The sea alters her character continuously, yet in this flux there is also constancy. From tiny storm petrels to majestic albatrosses, graceful tropic birds to mighty blue whales, all represent the enduring spirits of the sea, the very essence of liberty. They move freely across the globe, with only a few continents to divert their wanderings through worlds made of water and sky.

BETWEEN THE SEA AND THE SKY
Michael Gore

Seabirds have always held a special appeal to mariners. They follow ships for hundreds of miles across the deepest regions of the oceans; flocks wheeling over the water indicate shoals of fish and the sudden appearance of inshore birds tells the mariner that he is approaching land. And, in times past they have provided a rich source of fresh food. "The Rime of the Ancient Mariner" by Samuel Coleridge, published in 1798, tells the tale of a sailor who commits a motiveless crime by killing a friendly albatross. After he repents, supernatural powers carry his ship home; but ever afterward he must do penance by teaching others to love and revere all things that God has created.

Sadly, the lesson was not learned. Since that poem was published, five species of seabirds have become extinct. Best documented is the great auk, the only flightless bird in the northern hemisphere. Fearless and helpless, it was herded into corrals and clubbed to death; the feathers were used for bedding, the carcasses for oil, and the eggs for food. The vast colonies dwindled rapidly and the last two known birds were killed by a fisherman on an island off the coast of Iceland on June 4, 1844.

Today, of the 312 species of seabirds, no fewer than 55 are classified as rare and endangered by the International Council for Bird Preservation, the United Nations' agency responsible for bird conservation.

Since conservation became a household word in the 1960s and people became aware of the need to preserve all species from the effects of human activity, the situation has much improved and efforts are being made to ensure that other species do not go the way of the great auk. Islands containing important seabird colonies have been purchased by conservation agencies to ensure that the birds are not disturbed during their breeding season; access to the huge colonies in Antarctica has been restricted and the killing of seabirds for commercial gain is a thing of the past.

But threats remain: Long-lining for tuna, particularly by Japanese and Korean fishermen, results in the death of many albatrosses each year; the birds swoop down on the bait as the lines are being strung-out, are hooked and drown. Oil spillage from tankers, particularly by unscrupulous captains who wash their tanks at sea to save the cost of doing so under controlled conditions in port, kills many auks and other seabirds. And, of course, the all-too-frequent accidental oilspills result in the deaths of tens of thousands of birds which become saturated with the oil so that they end up waterlogged or poisoning themselves in their efforts to clean off the mess.

Rosy-lipped batfish. Cocos Island, Costa Rica. © **Birgitte Wilms**

Seabirds comprise a wide range of bird species. Many, such as the albatrosses, tube-noses (petrels and shearwaters), gannets, frigate birds, and auks spend all their lives at sea except for the short time they are nesting and rearing young. Others, such as some of the gulls, cormorants, and pelicans spend more time close to shore, some of them being common around our coastal towns. But all 312 birds classified as seabirds are defined as birds whose normal habitat and food source is the sea, whether this be coastal, offshore or pelagic, or at certain times of the year the sea is their habitat choice and principal source of food.

The main concentrations of seabirds are in the colder northern and southern regions, with the greatest numbers in the south. There, where there are few predators, they are found in great numbers. Colonies of breeding seabirds can be immense; in the Falkland Islands, one colony of black-browed albatrosses, almost certainly the bird killed by the ancient mariner, numbers 140 000 pairs, almost a quarter of the world population. This is a huge concentration of large birds which can only survive because of an abundance of squid, small fish, and krill in the nutrient-rich waters around the Islands.

Some penguin colonies are similarly huge: Adélie and chinstrap penguin colonies on islands off the Antarctic Peninsula number well over 100 000 pairs. Krill is their main source of food and there is an abundance of these tiny shrimps, the total population of Antarctic krill being estimated at 600 000 billion, weighing more than the whole human race! But humans are already starting to harvest krill and with modern fishing technology, even with the present abundance it is not inconceivable that the survival of the seabirds —not to mention that of the great whales which rely on krill as their main source of food— could be threatened by overexploitation.

In the colder waters of the northern hemisphere, huge colonies of gannets nest on rocky islands and guillemots and razorbills breed on sheer cliff faces, hundreds often crowded together on one ledge. Puffins, auklets, and shearwaters nest in burrows or in crevices under rocks on remote islands, many in large colonies.

Among the seabirds are several which are in the *Guinness Book of Animal Records*: The wandering albatross has the longest wings of any bird, with a total wingspan of 11.5 feet (3.6 meters); the arctic tern migrates further than any other bird, from the Arctic, where it breeds, to the Antarctic during the northern winter;

and Wilson's petrel, a tiny tube-nose about the size of a swallow, which nests in crevices on islands all around the Antarctic continent, is considered to be the world's most abundant bird; when seen fluttering over the water feeding on krill, it is hard to believe that these birds are in fact superb long-distance flyers which almost equal the Arctic tern in their migrations, moving from the Antarctic to spend the southern winter as far north as Newfoundland and Ireland.

Unlike northern breeding birds, many of which migrate south with the exception of Wilson's petrels, few southern seabirds move north beyond the equator, although many range great distances across the southern seas. There are occasional reports of southern birds occurring in northern waters, but most probably refer to birds which have hitched a lift on a steamer along the way.

Of the 55 seabirds considered to be endangered, several are extremely vulnerable because their numbers are low and they occur in only one or two locations. The Amsterdam albatross, which is confined to Amsterdam Island in the southern Indian Ocean, has a population of less than 70 birds with only five pairs breeding annually on average. Human activity, the draining of peat bogs, and introduced cattle (which trample the nests), cats, and rats are considered the causes of their decline. Their breeding area has been fenced off to keep out the cattle and strenuous efforts are being made to build up the population. The Bermuda petrel was thought to be extinct until rediscovered in 1951, when a small colony of 18 pairs was found; today, as a result of careful management, they number about 50 pairs. The Más a Tierra petrel, with a total population of a few hundred pairs on three islands off the west coast of South America, suffers predation by feral cats and rats, which pose a threat to wildlife on many isolated islands. Perhaps another 15 species are so endangered.

As has been proven only too frequently in the past, humans and their introduced animals can quickly eradicate a species. More enlightened attitudes, which have developed over the last 30 years, will hopefully ensure that we do not repeat the mistakes of the past, so that the mariner far from land will still be able to touch his cap at the albatross following in the wake of his boat and look wistfully at the shearwater soaring effortlessly over the waves; the penguins will continue to make their epic journey across the ice to catch food for their young, and all the other seabirds which make up such an important part of our avifauna will continue to flourish.

Wandering albatross. South Georgia Island, UK. © **Frans Lanting**/Minden Pictures

ON THE FRONTIERS OF KNOWLEDGE
Jorge Soberón

"The Earth looks like a glowing blue ball on black velvet!" exclaimed commander Frank Borman from the Apollo 8 capsule, some 380 000 kilometers from the globe. The extraordinary view that the commander had can be explained if we take into account that 71% of the Earth's surface is covered by oceans, which occupy a volume 18 times greater than the total of the landmasses that emerge from the oceans' surface, totalling 360 million cubic kilometers of water.

Referred to in ancient times as the "seventh continent," the ocean constitutes not only the oldest of all ecosystems, but also the largest. It represents an effective living space that is much more extensive than that available on the surface of the continents. It is a mine that concentrates all the elements and compounds identified by chemistry, metals such as gold, diverse organic matter, and extremely varied flora and fauna. Moreover, it has impressive "seascapes" dominated by enormous mountain ranges, great volcanic cones or hydrothermal shafts; with a global system of currents comparable to the winds we find over land, tides produced by the gravitational pull of the Moon and the Sun on the Earth, and a countless number of wonders, nuances, sizes, shapes, and colors that reflect its majesties.

Life emerged from the seas some 4 500 million years ago. Thus, evolution began in the oceans long before it occurred on land, and life remained confined to them for approximately ninety percent of the time that has elapsed since its origins. The biodiversity existing in the ocean and on land presents interesting contrasts: of all the species that have now been identified, less than 15% are in the ocean; nevertheless, of the 33 known phyla of animals, 32 are present in the marine environment (21 of which are only found in the ocean) and only 12 on land. Could this great difference in species be a real phenomenon or merely a product of our ignorance?

The structure of biological communities is also very varied. For example, in the tropical rain forest, which is the terrestrial ecosystem that is the richest in species, the predominance of plants is obvious, and vertebrates tend to be much less conspicuous. On the contrary, in a coral reef the presence of vertebrates is immediately

apparent, as well as that of a countless number of invertebrates of all types. What are the ecological reasons for these differences?

Different reasons have been adduced for these contrasts, yet no consensus has been reached; what cannot be denied is that one of the most significant differences between the land and the ocean is the lack of information on marine organisms, which obliges us to intensify studies of them, as well as suitable planning of the use of those organisms.

The century of discoveries and major land conquests officially ended in 1958, at the close of the International Geophysical Year, when the map of the world was completed. However, humankind has never lost its spirit of exploration and, therefore, knowledge of the oceans and of the life forms that inhabit them is expanding rapidly. Humans sail on better and more equipped vessels; submarines reach depths heretofore unimaginable; a great number of live organisms is identified, from microscopic ones to the largest mammals that ever lived on the planet. In turn, the use of marine resources in all aspects of humans' lives is diversified and intensified, to the extent that nowadays humans depend greatly on the items produced from resources obtained from the sea.

These are the reasons, both the scientific and more pragmatic ones, that make this book, within the framework of the International Year of the Ocean, a way of uniting and disseminating the knowledge we have on the marine environment and its resources, in order to comprehend the ocean as part of the world and to utilize it intelligently for the benefit of humankind. It also serves as an invitation to explore the mystery and beauty of the seas, without losing sight of the vulnerability of the life forms they contain.

TIME ON ICE
Christine Eckstrom

I am walking on the surface of the Southern Ocean. Antarctica is ten miles to the south. The surface is a layer of sea ice, attached to the continent. In winter, the ice freezes out from the coast in a slow, white wave; in summer, it recedes and breaks

Gray-headed albatrosses. South Georgia Island, UK. © **Frans Lanting**/Minden Pictures

up. I have come here by helicopter from an icebreaker docked twenty miles north, where the ice meets the open sea. I can't stay long. It's late spring, and the surface is starting to melt. Big cracks run through the ice like lightning bolts. Across them meander the tracks of penguins, leading north to the sea. High above, streamers of cirrus arc across the sky, a sign that wind is coming.

The landscape around me looks like a fairy-tale painting of heaven. I am encircled by an archipelago of mountainous ice islands. They rise several hundred feet, some grouped in ranges, others alone. They are blue in shadow, snow-white in sun, with deep crevices in their walls that reveal an interior of denser ice the color of brilliant turquoise. The mountains emerge from a white plain of sea ice that stretches to every horizon, leading to more blue-ice mountains far in the distance. By midday the sun has melted a thin veneer from their walls, and the mountains shine like pearl essence, lustrous and liquid, making them seem even more imaginary and impermanent than the ice under my feet.

This is the real illusion: Everything here looks like land, but it is all made of water. I am walking on the frozen skin of the ocean. The mountains are made entirely of ice. They are icebergs that calved from an ice shelf to the east, drifted west with the coastal current, and grounded here on the continental shelf. They are trapped in the same sea ice that supports me. Each winter, the ring of ice that forms around Antarctica grips this archipelago of icebergs into place. When the sea ice melts in summer, the icebergs are freed. They shift and roll, until winter holds them fast again. Every year this world is rearranged in a new geography, as if you could watch Earth's tectonic history in fast motion.

Up close, the ice mountains have the geology of landforms layered like ancient canyon walls, fractured with fault lines, slit with tall needle's-eye clefts. There are tabletop mesas and high spired peaks and deep caves hung with icicle stalactites in neat rows, like whale baleen. Several mountains have thin meltwater falls, and one has, at its base, a small pool where emperor penguins are splashing like children.

The emperors slosh in the pool in excited, bobbing mobs. Others line up at the edge and belly flop in. Farther out, more emperors approach in loose lines, tobogganing on their bellies down a long canyon that leads to the pool. At the other end of the canyon, a mass of emperor chicks clusters at the base of a blue-ice wall. From a distance they look eerily like people. Most are teenagers, appearing awkward and half-dressed as their feathers molt in illogical, artless patterns. Other ones, a little younger, are still precious in puffed coats of fluffy chick down.

This iceberg archipelago is a traditional nesting site, one of only forty known emperor penguin colonies found around the rim of Antarctica. More than twelve thousand breeding pairs gather here each year, and among the blue-ice mountains stretching into the distance are more chicks, perhaps seven thousand in all, scattered in broad, gray patches like shadows on the ice.

Being among emperors, watching the smooth regularity of their movements, is mesmerizing and calming. They move with steady composure, stoic and unflustered, with a serene demeanor that belies the extremes of their lives. Their annual cycle is a race against ice and time. Emperors are the largest of penguins, nearly four feet tall, weighing ninety pounds, and they need more time than any others to raise their young. For their chicks to mature before the ice breaks up, emperors must breed in the Antarctic winter. In late autumn, when other penguins and seabirds head north, emperor penguins turn south, facing into the maw of the cruelest season. They trek in from the sea and across the ice to traditional colonies at the edge of the continent. There each female lays a single egg, transfers it to her mate, and leaves for the open sea. The males huddle together, eggs balanced on their feet, incubating through two months of darkness and gales. The chicks hatch in mid-winter. On miraculous cue, the females return to feed them and relieve the males, who have lost nearly half their body weight. For five more months the parents journey like marathon athletes, back and forth across a hundred miles of ice to the sea, shuttling food to their young. The chicks must fledge by mid-summer, when the sea ice literally melts out from under their feet. Otherwise they won't survive.

In full sun, the ice is showing signs of rot. Holes pock the crust like a moth-eaten rug. By late afternoon, I punch through to my knees.

I sit down near the chicks, listening to their chirping soprano whistles as they plead to their parents for more food, even as their bellies sag, pear-shaped, to the ground, so full they can hardly waddle. A few older chicks try to make the stuttering

Emperor penguins. Weddell Sea, Antarctica. © **Frans Lanting**

nasal trumpet calls of adults, but their voices crack. In the distance, long skeins of adults toboggan across the ice plain to the open sea, still foraging for their young. Without turning to look, I hear them passing behind me. I sense the soft crunch in the ice as each rear foot pushes off, pedaling evenly, rhythmically, over the white plain.

Emperor penguins are birds born of blizzards, progeny of ice. They may be the truest of seabirds, never touching land in their lives. Their fate is tied to ocean, weather, season, ice, to this ephemeral geography.

An ice column falls and booms like a cannon, echoing down the walls of the canyon. The evening air is cold, but the landscape is dissolving. The ice mountains are dripping. The ocean is nearer. In a week or two, the young ones will be carried out to liquid sea on floes of sea ice, broken pieces of this old geography. The ocean will lap here where I stand, erasing everything but the memories of the emperors.

A FUTURE FOR OUR MARINE WORLD
Stanton A. Waterman

It is not fashionable these days to express any optimism about the world's environment, either terrestrial or marine. It seems to me that we ask for negatives in the news and thrive on depressing events. So that when I read about what is happening to the environment, I search in vain for any encouragement.

I am an optimist by instinct and so have taken note of some optimistic signs that we are at least slowing down our hellbent course of destruction of our global environment. To me, the most obvious sign is our own national awareness of the problems, an awareness that has more recently spread to most of Western Europe and is beginning to have an impact on some of the Third World countries. My interest is, of course, particularly directed to the sea. Cousteau, son and father, have focused on the problems that assail our water-planet and perhaps reached the largest number of people with their message of concern and care. They, more than any, have gone beyond the relatively small world of divers to alert a broad, international public. And today every underwater film festival and symposium and every dive-related publi-

cation is characterized by conservation motifs. So we are aware. We are not dead in the water. But how are we giving awareness the name of action? I have observed some positive action in places where it counts.

My profession is making underwater films and videos; so I am naturally most concerned with the tropical reefs on which I do most of my work. As sport diving increased, the damage to reefs from anchors could have become critical, especially in areas of the world where dive tours have proliferated. Bonaire in the Netherlands Antilles was one of the first popular Caribbean diving locations. About thirty years ago, Capt. Don Stuart, the man who developed popular diving there, was the first to establish permanent moorings at the most frequented dive locations. Since that time all the most popular dive locations in the Caribbean as well as in the Western Pacific have adopted this excellent practice.

An example of terrible attrition by anchoring is the destruction of large areas of reef at Grand Cayman by the big oceangoing cruise boats. The drag of their huge anchor chains across the coral as the ships swing cuts a swath of destruction greater than a football field. I have dived those areas. They are a wasteland and will take a generation or more to even partially recover. The Cayman Government is pressing the cruise operations to install permanent moorings and will ultimately succeed.

In the Caribbean, the most popular islands for diving have long since formed Dive Boat Operators Associations and established guidelines for the operators. Divers are directed to take absolutely nothing from the reefs and to avoid even touching the reefs with their fins or bodies. These directives are enforced by the dive guides themselves and —in many places— enforced by a staff of Marine Environment Wardens, backed by their governments with a mandate to arrest and fine. Among the places in the Caribbean that have initiated such protective measures are the Cayman Islands, Bonaire, The Bay Islands, Curaçao, and Belize.

The live-aboard dive boats on which I host tours in the Caribbean and off the coasts of Central America, as well as Hawaii, Fiji and Micronesia, are equipped with holding tanks for their effluence. No longer are the wastes from those boats discharged onto the reefs or into the open sea.

It is beyond my scope to discuss the range of conservation actions here in North

America that have been encouragingly effective. Salmon have returned to our rivers and lakes. Fish stocks are increasing through controls on wasteful practices in commercial fishing (i.e., gill netting) and government legislation has been enacted to reduce the harvest of depleted species and protect endangered ones. There is no longer an open season on sharks. On our coasts, the commercial harvesting of sharks is now tightly controlled. Perhaps the most amazing indication of an awareness by civilized nations of the value of all marine animals in the balance of the marine ecosystem is the legislation by South Africa and also by Australia to protect the great white shark, *Carcharodon carcharias*, the subject of the novel *Jaws*, and the most feared of all sharks.

Conservation as a force in our lives is so recent that it is less than a generation old. It is largely embraced now by the Western world and the more affluent countries, but the premise of restraint today for security tomorrow is not viable in poor countries where fishermen can barely support their growing families day-by-day with what they can harvest from a fishing ground that has been steadily and recklessly plundered by generations before them.

I lived, along with my family, with a family of poor fishermen on an island in French Polynesia some years back. I watched the fishermen poison the reefs with a native root called *timba*. All fish on the reef succumbed to the poison —butterfly fish, wrasses, parrot fish, damselfish—, most too small to be eaten. The activity was illegal then and is now. It is still going on and there is no way the French government can police the far-flung islands.

In the Philippines, I watched the indentured child divers, called *muruami*, sweep over a reef, about thirty of them in a line across the entire reef, and drive the fish into a waiting net. Nothing that moved remained. The reef was swept clean, and the pirate junk on which they lived moved on to other reefs in the area. Again, the activity was illegal. In the vast archipelago of islands that compose the Philippines, enforcing the law was impossible. There are such examples all over the Third World, where subsistence living is the level of the economy.

I always look to the bottom line and there I see population; too many human beings in a closed, encapsulated ecosystem with diminishing resources. A philosophical cartoon character said: "We have found the enemy, and it is us."

Education can help; the promotion of respect in a young generation for Nature, for the environment we share with all life on the planet, can help. I have at times used a quotation that perhaps best expresses my thoughts. It was written by Henry Beston, a Harvard naturalist. He wrote:

"We need a newer and a wiser and a more mystical sense of the animal. Remote from universal Nature and living by complicated artifice, man in civilization regards the animals through the glass of his knowledge and sees thereby a feather, greatly magnified, and the whole image in distortion. We patronize them for their incompleteness, for their tragic fate in having been formed so far below ourselves; and thereby we err, and greatly err. For the animal shall not be measured by man. In a world older and more complete than ours, they live finished and complete, gifted with extensions of the senses we have lost or never attained, living by voices we shall never hear. They are not brethren. They are not underlings. They are other nations, caught with ourselves in the net of life and time, fellow prisoners of the splendor and the travail of the Earth."

THERE IS HOPE FROM THE SEA
Mark Van Putten

There is hope from the sea, but none from the grave.
IRISH PROVERB

The Earth's seas, the watery womb of all life, yield up their secrets slowly. We have been forever spellbound by the ocean's beauty (reflected in the book you're holding), awed by its power, enchanted by that which lies fathoms-deep, near the Earth's primordial core. Once as seemingly impenetrable as outer space, the ocean's depths still harbor mysteries that elude our most advanced technologies. "New" forms of life spew from fissures in the ocean floor; unique chemicals with great potential for medicinal use are found in coral reefs.

Although the seas seem eternal, as we now know in this international "Year of the Ocean," they are not indestructible. Dependent on the global ocean for our very existence, we mindlessly abuse it, regularly dumping into it millions of gallons of

Gooseneck barnacles. British Columbia, Canada. © **Jason Puddifoot** spilled petroleum products, mountains of garbage, nuclear and medicinal waste, and direct and diffuse releases of chemical toxics. The ocean's very vastness lulls us into believing that it has an infinite capacity to absorb the refuse and detritus of human activity. It does not.

The reality is that some of our seas and the life they support are already dying. The Black Sea is so polluted that it is fast becoming a watery grave, decreasingly capable of supporting aquatic life, a fishing industry or even recreation. Unless environmental abuses are reversed, it will surely become another "Dead Sea."

Many of the initiatives to save our oceans parallel the National Wildlife Federation's efforts to curb water pollution, writ large. Examples include our work to stanch the flow of toxic effluents from strip-mining operations into water resources vital to people and wildlife. We've also launched "Saving Our Watersheds," an ambitious program to control "invisible" sources of pollution such as nutrient runoff and airborne toxics that threaten inland and coastal waters alike.

As this beautiful volume reminds us, we must not allow poisonous waste and other abuses such as overfishing —the strip mining of the seas— to despoil and unbalance the world's largest ecosystem, the very source of life itself. Rather, we must link arms to ensure that the global ocean remains a sustainable habitat for marine life, as well as a source of sustenance, wonder, and beauty for generations to come.

RECREATION FOR THE EYE AND THE MIND
Michael Small

It is five thirty a.m. on an April morning, and we are anchored beside Isla Jicarita, an islet fringed with orchids off the Pacific coast of Panama. Daylight is breaking on the horizon to the east. I drop down fifteen meters to the sandy bottom under the boat, and adjust my eyes to the faint light from overhead. Getting my bearings, I look around to read the bottom. It is flat, undulating sand in all directions. I set off, finning two meters off the bottom scanning the terrain, until I come to an area

where waves of coarser sand are piled up in "dunes" about a foot high. I line myself up along one of the dunes and follow its length, until I see what I have been told to look for: a curving mound of piled-up sand running counter to the grain of the dune. I follow this short mound to the end, and reach down and dig. A magnificent, hard, smooth, shiny shell pops up —the porphyry olive, the largest species of its kind in the world. Its six-inch, bullet-shaped shell, in chocolate brown decorated with pink triangles, is spectacular, but the animal that made it is even more impressive. It has a wide, soft, caramel-colored foot that comes to a head with two eyestalks and a probing siphon. When returned to the sand, the animal quickly starts to dig, disappearing from the rising light overhead until only the siphon remains, peeking up through the sand.

Four years later and on the other side of the Pacific, I am sitting in a Zodiac at night with a demented Australian diver, speeding over a lagoon in the Russell Group —a cluster of low, swampy islands in the central Solomon Islands. We reach the edge of the reef and tie off to a nearby coral head. We backflip over the side of the Zodiac into the black water, and start heading down a sheer coral wall. And down. And down. At forty meters, my partner disappears. Alone, hovering in empty space, in the dark with only my dive light, and feeling the early effects of nitrogen narcosis, I start to ascend. I begin looking carefully in all the pockets and crevices and find that in this vertical environment, mollusks congregate in the few flat ledges of sand. There are tented cone shells out hunting for small fish; shiny cowries feeding on small sponge patches; and spiny murex shells, out hunting other mollusks, whose shells they can bore through with their hard, radular tongues. Suddenly, my missing partner appears to my right. He has pushed the limits of the envelope by heading down to fifty meters to check out the walls of a deep reef cave for the elusive princely cowrie. After twenty-eight years in the Solomon Islands, he has found only three of these shells. Tonight was not one of those nights, so we complete the dive in peace, pausing to exhale our accumulated nitrogen in the shallows as we enjoy watching the reef come alive at night.

I view the sea through the lens of conchology; and conchology takes you to strange places —where ordinary sport divers and photographers would never choose to go. In the galaxy of humans' pursuits underwater, it may seem to be a narrow interest. In fact, it involves studying one of the great phyla of the animal kingdom —the mollusks—, which are found at all depths and in all habitats, which come in myriad colors, shapes and forms, and whose ground-up shells constitute much of the world's beaches.

The first book ever written on conchology, by an Italian priest in the seventeenth century, was called *Recreation for the Eye and the Mind*. It is still an apt description. Conchology does require sharp eyes. Most mollusks are nocturnal and hide themselves under rocks, beneath the surface of the sand, or deep inside coral during the day. To see many of them, you usually have to dive at night, when they cautiously come out to feed. Conchology also requires an ability to read the bottom, to spot the specific habitats and microenvironments in which mollusks live. And in the name of recreation, it requires a willingness to go places other people would not go, and do things other people would not do. I once was camping on the beach of an uninhabited island in Malaysia. A sharp squall came up at night and a hard rain started blowing across the bay. Everyone else in our group of divers retreated to their flimsy tents. My dive buddy and I immediately pulled on our dive gear and headed for the open water. Above, the rest of our party were cold, wet and miserable. Twenty meters below, the sea was still, warm, and the harp shells were out feeding on the sand. It was the right place to be at the time.

Conchology also exercises the mind. Like any branch of biology, it is grounded on taxonomy and history —the history of humans' attempts to catalog life in the sea. It is not always easy to identify what you find. Many families of mollusks have been poorly described; many more have been poorly illustrated. Many species come in multiple varieties and can form hybrids with neighboring species. To judge whether a given shell belongs to one species or another, you often have to know where it came from, what depth it lived at, what bottom it was living on, and make adjustments for all of these factors against the original type description —which is often based on an eighteenth-century woodcut, or a nineteenth-century

hand colored engraving, rather than a sharp twentieth-century photograph. For many mollusks there is a welter of duplicate names and competing descriptions, often backed up by competing egos among the malacologists who named them. I know people who make a specialty of historical malacology —tracking down the original types and descriptions of mollusks and then sifting out all the subsequent claims to have named the same shell. Entering these murky academic waters unprepared can be more dangerous than looking for the mollusk itself in its marine environment.

Finally, conchology provides a practical education in biodiversity. It trains you to view the planet from the perspective of the oceans that unite us, rather than the borders that divide us. Mozambique and Hawaii lie at the opposite ends of the mighty Indo-Pacific faunal province —yet they have more in common, in terms of their mollusk life, than Hawaii does with any of the other forty-nine states in the U.S. Meanwhile, a short stretch of coastline from southern California through northern Baja California constitutes a faunal province of its own. It had the richest abalone population in the world in terms of population density and species diversity; but this magnificent resource has long been under pressure from commercial collectors, sport divers, and coastal development. The advent of a lethal abalone virus has pushed one beautiful California species, the white abalone, to the brink of extinction, and most of the others are threatened. Yet apart from a handful of conservationists and conchologists, no one else seems to care about the fate of these lowly invertebrates.

Conservation is the common responsibility of everyone who enjoys the sea. The diversity of life in the oceans, celebrated in this book, makes possible a diversity of human approaches to the ocean —as a source of livelihood, recreation, education, and sheer wonder. The photographs in this volume make visible what has been invisible to the great majority of people who have never seen life underwater. Without their support for marine conservation, future generations will never have the opportunity I have had to find a personal niche in the web of life in the sea.

Nautilus. Palau, Micronesia. © **Norbert Wu**

IMAGES OF THE SEA
Martha Hill

Planet Earth is misnamed. It should be Planet Ocean. We need only look at a globe, and see how much of it is colored blue, to realize the significance of the oceans to our world. Occupying three quarters of the Earth's surface, they remind us that a good part of it is an uninhabitable, aqueous expanse. How vital are these immense bodies of water? We are just on the cusp of understanding their importance.

We humans are land-loving, air-breathing, unflippered mammals. For most of us, the sea represents an alien, even hostile environment. In the last few decades, we have finally overcome this fear and ventured underwater to explore the lightless depths. For years, we had only traveled above the surface of the seas. Now, only as the twentieth century reaches its close, are we traveling into and underneath the oceans to explore them as fragile and complex ecosystems in their own right.

Fortunately, the oceans have remained international bodies, free of ownership by any one nation. However, as such, they have been ripe for plundering by all. Overfishing, mining, oil extraction, pollution, ozone-depletion, and river disturbance are very real threats to marine environments everywhere. In the last decade, we have come to understand their pivotal role in the climate of this planet, when a single warm current, such as El Niño, can disrupt weather patterns all over the world.

For me, as a child, the most potent images of the sea were principally the paintings of Winslow Homer. His magnificent oils evoked the infinite power of the ocean —waves crashing on rocky shores, lonely fishermen in dories vulnerable to the capricious elements, an escaped slave on a raft in the middle of the sea, terrifyingly surrounded by sharks. Even in Homer's time, the late 1800s, post-Industrial Revolution, the sea still represented a dangerous environment for humans— a wild, unpredictable force as yet untamed by our technologies.

Now, thanks to such inventions as the camera and the aqualung, we have a new kind of ocean imagery. Underwater photographers capture glimpses of a most fantastic and intimate nature —colorful, otherworldly creatures, mysterious life forms from the depths of the ocean floors, social interactions of marine mammals and fishes— things most of us will never get to see firsthand. Underwater photography is truly a frontier in the overall field of nature photography.

In my years as Picture Editor of *Audubon* magazine, I understood the need for powerful imagery. We looked for photographs that carried a message. Normally, that message was part of a story, and often the pictures were used to illustrate specific points in that story. Since the magazine was the publication of a national conservation organization, we had a mandate to report on issues that would be of interest to our membership.

Another more subtle mandate was to inspire our members toward activism on behalf of the cause —in our case, conservation of animals and habitat, principally birds. To this end, we solicited the most beautiful imagery of the natural world we could find. By featuring stunning photographs, we hoped to encourage the desire to keep such beauty an integral part of our lives.

Imagery carries within it a power that words alone cannot sometimes deliver. Homer's paintings are certainly evidence of that. With photography, there is an even more convincing visual power —the eyewitness recording of something actually seen— that is, the power of truth. All editorial publications rely on this power of truth to strengthen their stories and underlying messages, whether it be documentary news reporting, science, consumer/special-interest journals or the ever popular how-to magazines. We tend to believe what we see, even though we may not always trust what we hear or read.

Evolutionary biologists tell us that life on the planet first began in its warm primordial seas, and that millions of years later, creatures crawled up on land, some eventually opting for a completely terrestrial existence. As you read through the pages of this beautiful book, remember that many of the subjects represented were unknown until this century. We are still piecing together this new knowledge to grasp the bigger picture. It may take us into the next century to fully comprehend the significance of marine environments to our overall survival. For me, it suffices to believe they are vital. And that is reason enough to want to safeguard their health.

Each of us should try to find a way of protecting the marine environment in our own personal spheres of activity. This might be something as simple as picking up the plastic bags and trash that litter beaches everywhere, or cutting apart the plastic loops that hold soda cans together. These items strangle and suffocate seabirds, turtles, and mammals all over the world. If we each do our part, we will help stem the tide of pollution and overexploitation that has been the history of humankind on this irreplaceable home we should be calling Planet Ocean.

Storm. California coast, USA. © **David Muench**

SONG OF THE OCEANS
Carlos Eyles

The entire range of living matter of Earth, from whales to bacteria and from oaks to algae, could be regarded as constituting a single living entity... endowed with faculties and powers far beyond those of its constituent parts.

SAMES E. LOVELOCK

The untamed world of the sea does not need humans, for it creates its own breath. And from that breath breathes the whale and the dolphin, who choose to breathe no other air. It is the breath of the wild. A wildness that once prevailed over the planet and gave richness and capacity for life; that nurtured all of humankind, who understood they could not exist in mind or body or spirit without the natural world to guide and renew them, and wash away their burgeoning civilization from time to time.

It has been a very long while since humankind has listened to the song of the natural world.

But not so very long ago, nor far away, our ancestors believed that the sea was a wide river which spilled along the shorelines and separated the land from yet more land in the unseen distance. Under this grand misconception they named the planet "Earth." Quite possibly, had they known the truth —that the water they believed to be a river was actually an ocean and that there were five oceans and countless seas—, they might have appropriately named the planet "Ocean."

This was the first of the great misconceptions regarding the oceans and seas of the planet Earth. More were to follow. In this century it was believed that the resources of the oceans were inexhaustible, and that they would supply a hungry world indefinitely. That the ocean could absorb with relative ease our poisons and toxins, our plastics and our petroleum, our refuse and sewage, industrial run-off and nuclear waste.

Despite these grand misconceptions and the inevitable truths that revealed them, humankind continues to tinker with the atmosphere, the earth and the water under the misguided belief that they can withdraw at any time and the planet will re-right itself, and all will be well again over time. These are delusions readily observed.

But what of that which is no longer readily observed?

What of the birthrights of all living things, and what of the miracles they produce, and of lessons taught and received, and of magic exchanged? What of renewal, and connection with the life-force on this sphere? This is the song that we do not hear, this is the song that has been forgotten.

Have we forgotten the obvious? Or is it just mislaid and, awaiting discovery, lies hidden in the clear light of day?

We are the offspring of the planet Ocean, and are inexorably connected to it by way of its liquid web. Our blood as much resembles sea water as our babies are able to swim from the moment of birth. When we are submerged, our heart automatically reduces its pulse rate from seventy to thirty beats a minute, something we share with whales, seals, and dolphins, but is not known to exist in any other land animal.

That which dwells beneath the sea is at the center of this living, liquid web, and must be cherished as precious for it is they —the animals and the creatures, the life-force of the oceans and seas— that carry their secrets and reveal their mysteries, and impart miracles so that we will not forget our legacy from nature and our responsibility to all living things.

The value of this life-force under the sea cannot be measured as a tangible resource, or as tonnage or profit. These inhabitants of the deep are nothing less than the trustees of the mystic, the holders of the last magic, and the keepers of the history of the planet Ocean and its song. To lose them is to render permanent destruction upon ourselves, and undo the web at its center, thus forfeiting our last opportunity for redemption, balance, and harmony that is our birthright in the natural world.

The essence of any living thing is the spirit of its life-force. This spirit is grandly displayed in the grace and exuberance of the dolphin at play, the whale in its breach, the fish in their flight. No other creatures express their freedom and sense of play more majestically than those who reside beneath the surface of the sea. It is this spirit that captures the human imagination, and indeed speaks directly to our souls. It is the simple delight of being alive that we instinctively are drawn to, and perhaps in the dolphins more than any other animal, we are re-

Puffin. Lundy Island, UK. © **John Cancalosi**

minded of the life of joy we have lost, given up, or betrayed in ourselves.

The waters of the planet should be as sacred to humans as they are to the humpback whale, for they are a precious thing that becomes more valuable with time. The oceans and seas must remain pure, and their inhabitants be allowed to live in peace, and be kept alive and healthy for our children and their children, for only their wild beauty can heal and renew when nothing else will.

It is said that the song of the humpback whale heals the wounds of the sea. It is hoped that it can heal the deep and abiding wounds of humankind as well, and perhaps some day we might once again understand its meaning.

THE CULTURE OF THE SEA
Enriqueta Velarde

Often, when I am on a boat sitting on the bow or bridge, or in a skiff, the image of the first men who set to sea comes to mind. I imagine them looking at the waters from a sandy beach, a windy cliff, or a primitive craft, bobbing up and down over fierce waves or floating serenely on a tranquil sea. That is how dozens of oceanic islands were settled, and useful plants were transported from one continent to another, and from a continental coast to that of an island. The human species evolved close to the sea and, as time went by, learned to take advantage of coastal and marine resources as food. Later, it also learned to use the sea as a channel for transportation, making use of floating objects —both natural ones and those made by humans themselves. In fact, no other anthropoid is able to swim like we are.

The knowledge that these cultures came to acquire about their natural resources made it possible to use them for thousands of years without depleting them. Admirably, the natives of the Pacific coast of Canada and California followed traditional norms that avoided overfishing; they conducted rituals related to marine and riverine fishes and mammals that ensured the abundance of these resources during the following season.

In the region of the Gulf of California where the Comcaac (or Seri) Indians fish,

there are five species of turtle. These marine reptiles are among the most important in the Seri's culture and world view. Their knowledge of these species is so extensive that they have fourteen terms to differentiate them, depending on their type or local variety, sex, age, reproductive or migratory status, or genetic variety. When one of these turtles was found on the beach or caught, it was not killed. Rather, a ceremony was organized in its honor and then it was released back into the sea.

The reasons why most riverine cultures have not overexploited their resources are many and varied. For example, the limited demand in the case of small human groups or a lack of fishing capacity. When a greater demand and fishing capacity came to be developed, these cultures established different methods for controlling fishing; among these are certain ritualized behavior patterns. An infinite range of fishing management techniques utilized by preindustrial peoples are based on the knowledge of the biological requirements of the species used. For example, the prohibition to fish during the spawning season, the fact that they do not fish all the individuals —especially those smaller than a certain standard size— or that they allow part of those caught to escape, limiting the number of traps or nets set in an area, or the use of certain tacit rules such as respect for whoever first arrived in a particular zone. Often, fishermen do not disclose their fishing sites other than to members of their own group. Many communities delimit areas or establish exclusive fishing rights. This is one of the most advisable methods, since it is much easier to distinguish a space used exclusively, as opposed to the resource per se, which in general is mobile. This form of fishing management was very common in countless cultures throughout the world, and can still be found among many peoples with an ancestral fishing tradition.

Another effective way to control fishing consists of diversifying the use of resources. Thus, fishing will involve many and not just a few species. However, at present, with rapid population growth and technological development, our needs and abilities to exploit and overexploit fishing resources have multiplied manyfold. One way of naturally regulating catches that was useful in the past and which currently is among the most effective ones is that of "lowest profitability." If the resource is so scarce that the expense necessary to catch it is greater than the profit, fishing be-

Osprey. Ojo de Liebre Lagoon, Baja California Sur, Mexico. © **Fernando Holschneider**/Sierra Madre

comes unprofitable. This form of control, although efficient in the long run, may turn out to be disastrous for the economy of a region if it takes place at crucial times, as was the case of Pacific sardine fishing on the Gulf of California in 1992, when a large part of the fishing fleet, as well as canning and processing plants handling this sardine, went bankrupt.

We still have a lot to learn, but past experience and traditional knowledge can help us so that we don't make the same mistakes in management that we have in the past. Modern-day fishing is "humankind's last great hunt." Major hunts on land have come to an end and now we are conducting them in the sea, an environment we are barely beginning to become familiar with.

When I spend several months on end working on an island, surrounded by hundreds of thousands of seabirds nesting —as I have done for the past twenty years— and experience the feeling one gets from these birds' vast energy, from realizing how their activity, actions, and achievements can give us an idea of what is happening in the sea, or gathering systematic information on their diet and breeding patterns, I understand how these seabirds, marine mammals or fishes have provided navigators and coastal inhabitants with information. Learning to interpret it, in an intuitive or empirical way or using the scientific method, and to employ it rationally, is part of our great endeavor as members of the community of inhabitants of this planet, call it Earth or Ocean, and of our responsibility as a "rational" species.

IN THE WAKE OF A WHALE
Michelle A. Gilders

The clouds are so low that they obscure the mountains, covering the snow that coats the peaks year-round: white on white. The water does nothing to brighten the scene. The Strait, which separates Bay from Passage from Ocean, is dark, steel gray and stippled with foam. Spray goes from the leading edge of wave to wave that breaks upon the surface, adding moisture to air already heavy with drizzle. The boat is jos-

tled like a person in an unforgiving crowd. Salty spray makes the deck slick. The undulating motion rocks and pitches the vessel, rolling it violently, and then pitches it bow first deep into the waves so that the prow disappears beneath several feet of cold and oppressive water.

None of this should have been too troublesome. I have been through far worse storms, where waves crashed over the ship's bridge, three stories high, and at night you had to strap yourself into your bunk to avoid an unceremonious ousting. Storms can be most invigorating when you allow your legs to absorb the impact of vessel versus water, and you breathe deeply a combination of salty water vapor and adrenaline. The problem on this occasion, surrounded by the eerily hidden mountains of Glacier Bay and Icy Strait in Southeast Alaska, is that as the prow is thrust into the frigid waters, I am riding it.

With the captain of the vessel safe and dry in the wheelhouse, I am directing our passage from the bow. My oilskins glisten in the rain, and every time the boat dips low into a wave, my feet and legs are immersed. The cold has an edge to it that penetrates to the core. My fingers hurt to move. Summer in Alaska can be far more glacial than temperate. It is usually at this point that memories of Tahitian atolls, Hawaiian beaches, and Caribbean sunsets come to the forefront of my mind, and I struggle to remember why I am putting my body through this punishment. Then the object of my particular obsession blasts from the water and neither the cold nor the wet seem to matter anymore.

There is magic in the substance of a whale: in its conformation, its attitude, and in its bearing. There is strength in its size, but it is carried with a quiet grandeur. There is no boasting in being a whale.

The weather did not bode well for whale-watching as we left Gustavus. The first hour of our voyage was uneventful, and the gray skies and sea hurt my eyes with their monotony. The mountains that surround these waters were invisible, vanished among the clouds as though they had never been. An explosion of white several kilometers distant changed the mood in an instant. The explosions continued. As we neared, the unmistakable form of a humpback whale, *Megaptera novaeangliae*, took shape, reaffirming that these gray seas hide marvels as great as the eye can behold.

Northern fulmar. Craileith Island, Scotland, UK. © **Francisco Márquez**

As the whale breached, its body arched in a sinuous curve. Water streamed from its throat grooves and off long, tapering pectoral flippers. The animal twisted in midair, falling on its back amidst boiling water of its own making. Seconds passed and the whale thrust its head up out of the water, lunging forward, once, twice, three times, four. Its head slapped heavily on the surface with cannon-like retorts. With a final lunge, the whale lifted its tail flukes and pounded the water's surface. Water sprayed forth. Apparently, tail-slapping matched head-lunging for the amount of fun it imparted, and the whale raised its tail repeatedly, beating the water into a maelstrom. It was an exhausting display to watch. I felt like cheering the whale on, encouraging its pageantry with exultations; with the wind tearing any sound from my lips before it reached my ears, I may have done just that. Without warning, the commotion ended. The whale fluked and dove.

All was quiet. The sound of the crashing whale was replaced by the wind. I took deep breaths. Three minutes passed, then five. I scanned around the boat, my zone of interest widening as more minutes passed. Seven minutes later the whale breached right in front of us. We had hardly moved. The breach was followed by head-lunges, three, four, five, then tail-slaps, then with a rounding of its vast humped back, the whale dove once again. Seven minutes later it breached. It was a routine and timing that it maintained for over an hour. The seven-minute breaks gave me the chance to return to the wheelhouse to change film out of the spray before going back to my wet perch in time for the next breach.

Why was the whale expending all that energy with such impressive leaps and displays above the waves? Was it sending a message to whales we could not see? Was it making a show for our vessel, or other distant ships? Or was it simply thrilling at the way it felt to jump clear of the water and land with a tremendous splash? And what was it doing for each of those seven minutes that it vanished beneath us? Was this whale playing hide-and-seek with us? Like a child jumping through puddles on a rainy day, the whale leapt over storm waves and plunged below them, perhaps marveling at the silence beneath the surge. This was a whale playing with an invisible friend or staging a fight with some unseen foe. This was exuberance magnified a hundredfold, and I felt privileged to have witnessed this fragment of a whale's life.

The oceans cover three quarters of our planet, and yet they remain alien to us. The majority of the world's human population lives within 160 kilometers of the coast, and yet the ocean is viewed as a barrier to be crossed, rarely a three-dimensional habitat to be explored. We make tentative excursions into the depths, expanding our knowledge with each voyage, but often we come back with more questions than answers; it seems that we can only catch rare glimpses of lives lived outside our own realm. We have learned most of what we know of cetaceans —length, weight, and their base utilitarian uses— from the destructive harvesting of whaling. But what of the minds that exist in the waters? The interactions between species? The evolutionary pressures that have fostered diversity? What of the simple wonder of the deep?

Four billion years ago, life began in the water. This aqueous medium, with its high specific heat and high density, is an ideal environment for life. Rich in the Earth's elements, seawater contains 84 of the 103 elements found on this planet. Water cradles life. It transports life amid vast currents and gyres that encompass the globe. These very same currents facilitated the movement of people from land to land, and fostered great cultures among island nations.

The oceans send forth rain clouds to wash the land, watering our crops with liquid and dissolved nutrients. They ameliorate our climate by absorbing the sun's heat and releasing it slowly, dampening the extremes. Waves redesign our coasts. Where rivers and oceans meet, vast deltas form to give a rich interface between land and sea.

Storms invigorate us when viewed from safety, and terrify us when not. Myths of ghost ships, vanishing vessels, mermaids, selkies, sea serpents, and torrential floods color the cultures of people wherever they have looked upon the infinite expanse and felt small or vulnerable. The ocean is contradictory. It is solace and threat. It is constant and changeable. It is all things at all times.

We treat the ocean as though it will always be there as it is today. But the history of whaling should serve as a warning. What we do not value above the purely utilitarian, we risk losing to those eager for quick profits, and that which we view as free and boundless is exploited without mercy. We may never regain the population of whales that once roamed the seas. With their removal, the balance of the ecosystem was changed, perhaps forever. What would the world be like without the blue

Humpback whale flukes. Southeast Alaska, USA. © **Jeff Foott** whale or the humpback? Without the yellowfin tuna or whale shark? What would the world be like without the Mona Lisa, the Pyramids, or countless works of art? If the objects that emerge from the human mind are invaluable, how much more important are those that can never be recreated or restored?

The oceans contain an estimated ten million species, although only 295 000 have been identified; ninety percent of the Earth's biomass resides in the sea. These numbers are suggestive of the importance of the blue-green, translucent, emerald, opaque gray, everchanging liquid that forms the heart of our misnamed planet, but still they cannot capture the inherent mystery of the ocean: the mystery that comes from watching a blue whale exhale a cloud of vapor nine meters high, from listening to songs sung in the dark depths, watching orca hunt fur seals on some remote beach, or the gentle interaction between a gray whale and its newborn calf.

The cold eye of science calls for the protection of the oceans for selfish reasons of human wants and needs, but in reality our obligation to conserve is both moral and personal. What do we risk losing if we do not? Forget for a moment that the oceans feed us, water us, and protect us from rising temperatures. They foster our imagination, they feed our spirit, and they enhance our cultures with myth and legend. They allow us to immerse our minds in the midst of creatures that are so different from the human, and yet that share an evolutionary heritage with our own species. The loss of a single one would diminish us all, for it would diminish some of the mystery of life itself.

The next time you marvel at the power of the ocean, the color of the water, the breaking of waves on a beach, or the brilliance of a sunset at sea, consider what lies just below the surface: the whales, the fish, the plankton. They may be out of sight, but they should never be forgotten.

Blue whale. California coast, USA. © **Doc White**/Earth Water Stock Photography

Lava flow entering the sea. Hawaii Volcanoes National Park, Hawaii, USA.
© **William Neill**

Kahoolawe and Molokai Islands. Hawaii, USA.
© **David B. Fleetham**/Silvestris

"Serene hours at the brief sunset, / when the sea embraces the sky / and the immortal hope is awakened / that when fire melts, fire it drinks."
Miguel de Unamuno.

"This grand show is eternal. It is always sunrise somewhere; the dew is never all dried at once; a shower is forever falling; vapor is ever rising. Eternal sunrise, eternal sunset, eternal dawn and gloaming, on sea and continents and islands, each in its turn, as the round earth rolls."
John Muir.

Blue whale. Gulf of California, Mexico.
© **Tui De Roy**/Auscape

Common dolphin. Fernandina Island, Galápagos, Ecuador.
© **Tui De Roy**/Minden Pictures

"There Leviathan / hugest of living Creatures, on the Deep / stretcht like a Promontorie sleeps or swimmes, / and seems a moving Land, and at his Gilles / draws in, and at his Trunck spouts out a Sea." John Milton.

"Remember what you have seen, because everything forgotten returns to the circling winds." Navajo proverb.

Sailfish. Cocos Island, Costa Rica. © **Jay Ireland** & **Georgienne E. Bradley**

"At about 40 feet we spotted a sailfish that dropped into the depths. When we looked up, another one was at the surface performing a territorial dance. Swimming in abrupt figure-eight formations, the great fish would flair its massive dorsal fin at each turn."

Jay Ireland & Georgienne E. Bradley.

Barracuda. Solomon Islands. © **Christopher Newbert**

"They poured from the surface like a waterfall. The barracuda numbered in the hundreds, and I watched them descend until my eyes couldn't follow them any longer." Birgitte Wilms.

Olympic National Park. Washington, USA.
© **Art Wolfe**

Bald eagle. Tongass National Forest, Alaska, USA.
© **John Hyde**/Wild Things

On the coast of Olympic National Park one can find endless beaches along-side majestic cliffs and huge forests. This site houses a great wealth of marine life, for even in a small pool formed by the tide one can find near-ly 4 000 organisms of 20 different groups, among them fishes, crabs, goose-neck barnacles, snails, globefishes, and sea anemones.

The oceans constitute an enormous source of food for hundreds of species of seabirds. Although this bald eagle is not considered a seabird, it is skill-ful at catching fish.

Southern elephant seals and king penguins. South Georgia Island, UK.
© **Art Wolfe**

"I love the contrast between the four penguins, seemingly oblivious to everything around them, and the elephant seals just behind them. It was an amazing moment, here one second and gone the next. It shows the power of the photograph to capture the 'decisive moment' for perpetuity." Art Wolfe.

Walrus bulls. Bering Sea coast. © **Tom** & **Pat Leeson**

"We were at this location for eight days, and during the nice weather (the first two days), there were about 500 walrus lounging on the beach. After several days of storm, the number fell to 150-200. This photo was taken on a rainy day. The steam or fog was caused by the rain falling on the warm bodies, which were all packed closely together." Tom & Pat Leeson.

Schooling bannerfish. Manado, Indonesia.
© **Fred Bavendam**/Minden Pictures

Green sea turtle. Hawaii, USA.
© **Doug Perrine**/Innerspace Visions

These fishes are clearly distinguishable from other similar species due to the long filament of their dorsal fin. They live around the reef, feeding on zooplankton and small invertebrates that live on the sea floor.

For 150 million years, sea turtles have lived in the oceans of the planet and nested on beaches in tropical and temperate zones. The eight species that exist in the world are threatened or endangered, since they are killed for their meat and their nests are pillaged. However, in many places new programs to ensure the future of these age-old creatures are under way.

Basking shark. Isle of Man, UK.
© **Jeremy Stafford-Deitsch**/ENP Images

Southern stingray. Los Roques Islands, Caribbean Sea, Venezuela.
© **F. Stuart Westmorland**

This gentle creature which is nearly 10 meters long and has tiny teeth swims in the waters near the surface with its enormous mouth open, feeding on millions of tiny crustaceans which it filters through its gills, the openings of which are so large that they practically encircle its entire body. Despite its imposing appearance, it is completely harmless due to its placid nature.

The stingray, which remains still and goes unnoticed until it moves short distances to feed or to escape from some intruder, swims away at a speed we wouldn't believe possible for a creature that spends most of its time resting on the ocean floor.

Orca. British Columbia, Canada.
© **Flip Nicklin**/Minden Pictures

Northern elephant seal pups. Año Nuevo Island, California, USA.
© **Frans Lanting**/Minden Pictures

"Amidst a play of lights and shadows, a fleeting silhouette appears, outlining its whimsical form of contrasts to conceal its presence under the tranquil surface of the ocean." Patricio Robles Gil.

In this photograph we see several flattened faces with great rounded eyes. These features remind us at times of our own species; the description of the elephant seal cannot be more exact than its name in Latin: *Mirounga angustirostris.*

Giant Pacific octopus. Northwest Pacific Ocean.
© **F. Stuart Westmorland**

Commensal fish with jellyfish. California, USA.
© **Richard Herrmann**

"The largest octopus species in the world. This big adult measured at least 5 meters from arm to arm. Despite its threatening appearance, it is practically harmless and almost always prefers to escape than to give battle to an uncertain enemy." F. Stuart Westmorland.

Moving about freely, thanks to the shelter they find among the tentacles of the jellyfishes, these small fishes apparently give their host nothing in return and, not content with that, also get a free ride with very little effort on their part.

Blue-footed boobies. Galápagos Islands, Ecuador.
© **Joe McDonald**

Common dolphins. Baja California, Mexico.
© **Joe McDonald**

"Following a school of fish, a large flock of blue-footed boobies, folding their wings and dropping like missiles, dove into the sea. The impression was organized chaos as birds moved in both directions at once."
Joe McDonald.

"From a distance the sea looked like it was boiling. There were several hundred dolphins swimming en masse, leaping out of the water with such rapidity that they resembled stones skipping across a quiet pond. In the half hour that we followed them, the dolphins changed direction several times, always in a group as they made their way across the sea."
Joe McDonald.

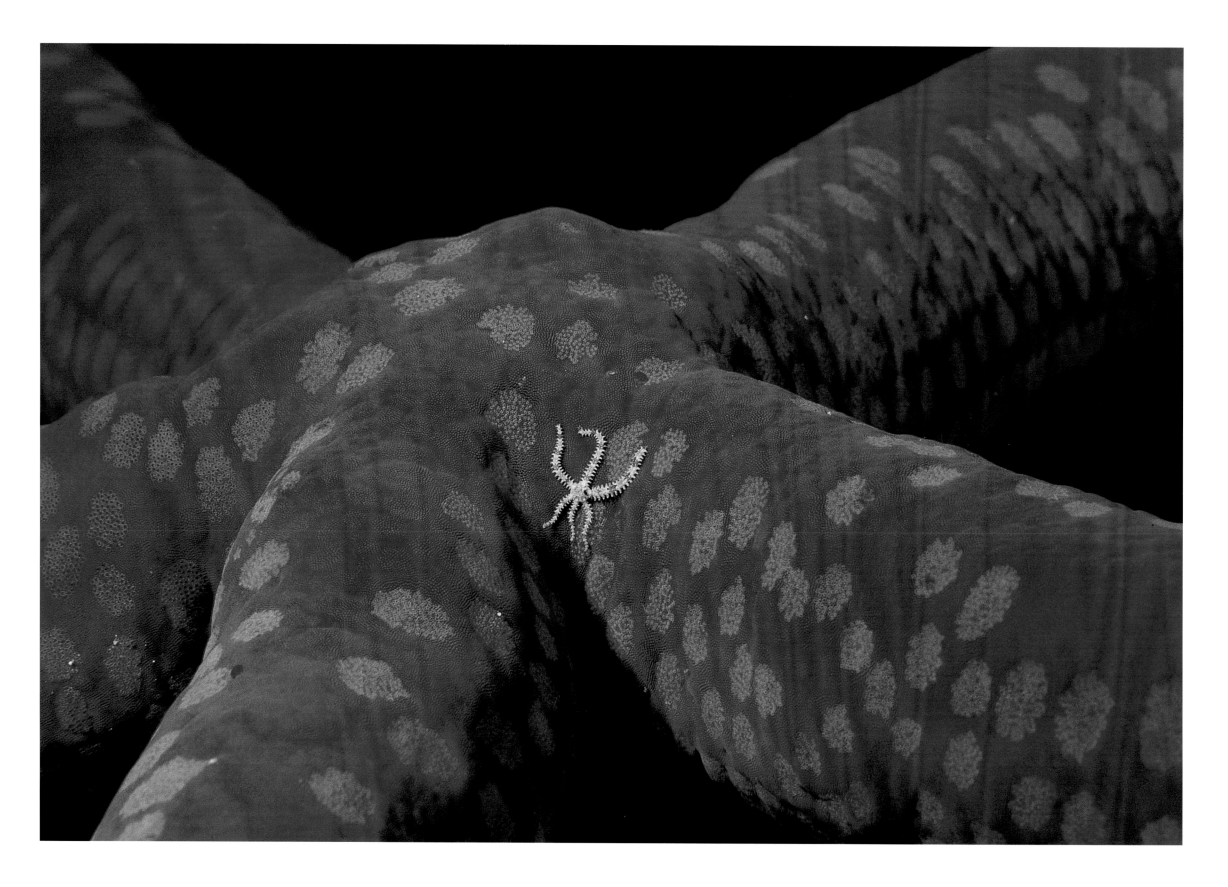

Pages 72-73

Humpback whale. Chatham Strait, Alaska, USA.

© **Thomas D. Mangelsen**

The first whalers called it "big wings" (Megaptera). Its leaps are as dramatic as they are unexpected, as if the whales were celebrating life with great, but brief leaps combining strength and grace.

Brittle star juvenile on a starfish. Solomon Islands.

© **Birgitte Wilms**

"Why is this starfish smiling? I can only speculate: other members of its family multiply by autonomous asexual reproduction. Interesting, but lonely. This one reproduces sexually by releasing eggs or sperm to mix randomly in the sea water, then producing planktonic larvae."
Birgitte Wilms.

Crown jellyfish. Red Sea.

© **Mike Bacon**

"While diving the north side of Big Brothers Island in the Red Sea at sunset, I encountered a strong current sweeping crown jellyfishes up from the abyss below. I quickly discovered I had just a few frames left on the roll and only moments of air before I had to return to the surface, much to my chagrin." Mike Bacon.

Adélie penguins. Hope Bay, Antarctic Peninsula.
© **Patricio Robles Gil**/Sierra Madre

"In our next to last day in the Antarctic, large groups of penguins were returning to land when they were propelled from the water, and fell all over each other. As photographers, we could not control our sense of anticipation and at times our laughter, like when a group fell on top of us." Patricio Robles Gil.

American white pelicans. Ojo de Liebre Lagoon, Baja California Sur, Mexico.
© **Patricio Robles Gil**/Sierra Madre

"There are some birds in the water called *atotolin*, which means water hen [...] it is said that it is the king of all the birds of the water [...] it has a wide mouth, sunk deeply to the neck, these birds fish with their mouths open or open their mouths like a fishing net, they are as large as a turkey; some of these birds are white and others are metal-colored." Fray Bernardino de Sahagún.

Beluga whales. Near Hudson Bay, Northwest Territories, Canada.
© **Tony Martin**/ENP Images

Young beluga riding on its mother's back. Somerset Island,
Northwest Territories, Canada.
© **Günter Ziesler**/Bruce Coleman, Ltd.

One of the most impressive sights in the animal kingdom is when hundreds of belugas gather together in the waters of a river in the Arctic, in Siberia, or in northern Canada. As the tide rises, whales begin to migrate upstream. Beluga is a Russian word which means white. However, their calves are born dark-colored and it isn't until they reach sexual maturity, at the age of 5 or 6 years, that they are transformed into the beautiful white whales of the North.

Black vulture and olive ridley sea turtle.
Santa Rosa National Park, Costa Rica.
© **Bill Curtsinger**

Olive ridley sea turtles. Nicoya Peninsula, Costa Rica.
© **Ryukichi Kameda**/Nature Production

The massive arrivals of sea turtles on beaches are legendary: this is a unique phenomenon in the reptile world. Thousands of them emerge from the sea to spawn, and each leaves nearly a hundred eggs buried in the sand. Later they return to the sea, never to see their young. When they come out of their shells, the baby turtles encounter a hostile world: on land they are confronted by birds, crabs, and small mammals, and in the sea by fishes and fishing nets. For that reason only 1% of them reach adulthood.

Soft corals and orange anthias. Red Sea.
© **Christopher Newbert**

Pyramid sea star. Galápagos Islands, Ecuador.
© **Doug Perrine**/DRK Photo

"The festive colors of soft corals and swirl of orange anthias make the reef appear like a country fair. The flowing current brings the sensation of an endless movement." Birgitte Wilms.

Sea stars scatter their reproductive cells in the water, just as some plants spread their spores in the wind. This is how their species has been perpetuated for millions of years, a fact that has been confirmed by studies of the fossils of these animals.

Polar bear cubs following mother. Wapusk National Park, Manitoba, Canada.
© Thomas D. Mangelsen

Arctic fox. Hudson Bay, Wapusk National Park, Manitoba, Canada.
© Thomas D. Mangelsen

"Their motion no longer warmed them and they shivered a little, the cold knifing noticeably down their throats with every breath. And still, could there be anything greater than this —chasing the big white bear over the top of the world?" Hans Ruesch.

In the Arctic Ocean, which is frozen for the most part, an Arctic fox is confused with the scenery thanks to its winter coat of fur, which helps it capture its prey, such as small ringed seal pups.

Southern giant petrel. Beagle Channel, Chile.
© **Tui De Roy**/The Roving Tortoise

Pacific white-sided dolphin. Vancouver Island, Canada.
© **Richard Herrmann**

On a windless morning, a southern giant petrel is gliding a few centimeters above the water. Except for the breeding season, these birds spend their entire lives at sea; they are adapted to "navigate" in the wind and even in the fiercest of storms they can be seen dancing in the air.

"During the fall and late summer, windless days can turn the surface of the water to glass in Johnstone Strait. These dolphins have been known to swim with, and harass the local resident orcas. However, the first sound of a transient pod of orcas sends them quickly swimming in the other direction." Richard Herrmann.

Sea anemone mouth (detail). Solomon Islands.
© **Burt Jones**/**Maurine Shimlock**/Secret Sea

"A coral reef, with its flamboyant colors and shapes, provides the clearest glimpse of the diversity and harmony of the ocean environment. A photograph like this one is a way to unlock the reef's hidden world of color, texture, and form." Burt Jones and Maurine Shimlock.

Boxer crab. Papua New Guinea.
© **Mike Bacon**

"Early one morning while searching under rocks in the shallows, I came face to face with a boxer crab defending its territory by waving small anemones grasped within each claw, hoping to ward me off. I could not help but admire the courage of this tiny crab striking a defensive pose against me." Mike Bacon.

Harbor seals. Elkhorn Slough, California, USA.
© **Frans Lanting**

Although seals' sense of sight is adapted to both in the water and outside it, their underwater vision is more specialized; they have huge eyes which allow them to see where there is little light, as is the case of the depths of the submarine world.

Sea otter eating crab. Channel Islands, California, USA.
© **Jeff Foott**

Despite their playful, comical manner, sea otters are highly specialized mammals adapted to marine life; their diet can vary greatly from one animal to the next, since each sea otter chooses its fare according to the invertebrates that are within its reach, such as crabs, snails, globefishes, octopuses, and abalones.

Skeleton Coast. Namib Desert, South-West Africa. © **Jim Brandenburg**/Minden Pictures

On the southwest coast of Africa, one of the most arid regions on this planet, rains are very scarce, but the cold current of the southern Atlantic condenses in the form of mist almost every night and bathes the desert as far as 100 kilometers inland. This moisture allows for the growth of plants which serve as sources of food for small insects to large mammals such as the giraffe.

Glacier. Anvers Island, Antarctica. © **D. Parer** & **E. Parer-Cook**/Auscape

The Antarctic is not only the coldest place on this planet, with temperatures reaching -89°C; it is also the largest surface on Earth that has remained pristine. Surrounded by one of the richest oceans, in the Antarctic is found 80% of all the fresh water on Earth, stored in its thousands of glaciers, some of them with a depth of up to two kilometers. All this impressive ice has accumulated for millions of years, since the Antarctic has so little precipitation that it would seem to be a desert.

Scenic reef. Red Sea.
© **Christopher Newbert**

"Around this undersea mountain, thick clouds of glassfish gathered, swirling in and out among the corals as if blown by strong winds. At night when they feed, the slightly luminescent green hue on their underside serves as a camouflage against the soft moonlight."
Christopher Newbert & Birgitte Wilms.

Sea whips. Solomon Islands.
© **Christopher Newbert**

"Preferring the deeper, cooler water with reduced sunlight, sea whips are beautiful in their own right and are often home to tiny gobies and shrimps. These tenants typically adopt the color of the coral they inhabit."
Christopher Newbert.

Nurse sharks. Florida Keys, USA. © **Nick Caloyianis**/National Geographic Society

"Locked in a turbulent embrace, two nurse sharks mate off the Florida Keys —the first time scientists have documented in detail the sex life of sharks in the wild. To subdue his partner, the male must seize the female's pectoral fin, flip her, and carry her from the shallows to deeper water."
Harold L. Pratt, Jr. & Jeffrey C. Carrier.

Dugong mother and calf. Shark Bay, Australia. © **Ben** & **Lynn Cropp**/Auscape

Dugongs, like manatees, are the only surviving members of their family. They are known as sea cows, since they are herbivorous mammals. They live in shallow seas in Southeast Asia and Australia, and can be found near the coasts.

Brown pelicans. Gulf of California, Mexico.
© **Fulvio Eccardi**

Magnificent frigate birds. Galápagos Islands, Ecuador.
© **Dieter** & **Mary Plage**/National Geographic Society

"In silent agreement and with harmonious synchrony, the brown pelican dives in search of anchovies and sardines. These gregarious birds, which breed in colonies, are among the most symbolic birds on the Gulf of California, which they cross from end to end guided by the more experienced among them." Fulvio Eccardi.

"...and when she goes there to where they breed, all the water birds also go after her, and they go towards the west." Fray Bernardino de Sahagún.

Emperor penguins. Cape Roget, Ross Sea, Antarctica.

© Graham Robertson/Auscape

Emperor penguins. McMurdo Sound, Antarctica.

© Bill Curtsinger

In the face of the strong winds and extreme temperatures typical of the Antarctic, emperor penguins have developed interesting adaptations. One is for some of them to huddle together to prevent heat loss. Another is the great density of their plumage, 80 feathers per square inch. Some researchers believe that when penguins submerge, the feathers act as little springs that withstand the compression, forming a layer of air that isolates them from the water and leaves behind a trail of bubbles.

Eroded iceberg. Gerlache Strait, Antarctica.
© **Joseph Van Os**

Southern right whale. Subantarctica, Argentina.
© **Doug Perrine**/Innerspace Visions

"In its endless circling through the biosphere, water flows constantly over every habitat and every life form, bathing and moistening, warming and freshing, nourishing and carrying away wastes."
Christopher N. Palmer.

The southern right whale was overexploited by whalers in the late nineteenth century. Hunting it was easy due to its great size and slowness, and its body contained so much oil that it floated even after it had died.
Thus its name is the right whale.

Tussock bird and southern elephant seal. Falkland Islands, UK.
© **Wayne Lynch**

Southern elephant seals and king penguins. Salisbury Plains, South Georgia Island, UK. © **Patricio Robles Gil**/Sierra Madre

This species of seal is the largest in the world. Males can reach a length of six meters and a weight of four tons, unlike females, who are only one quarter as long. On this page, we can see how a tussock bird feeds on the molted skin of a southern elephant seal; on the opposite page, a male whose demeanor indicates a warning. In both images we can observe the dimensions of these marine mammals, in contrast to the size of the birds accompanying them.

Gray reef sharks. Bikini Atoll, Pacific Ocean.
© **Steve Drogin**/Innerspace Visions

Just as the rattlesnake warns us that it is angry by the sound it makes, the gray reef shark arches its body and, swimming in an erratic fashion, would appear to be saying to anyone who dares to enter its domain that he or she is on the verge of being attacked.

Ocean sunfishes. San Diego, California, USA.
© **Richard Herrmann**

"I have been photographing ocean sunfishes in the open sea for 10 years now. I have seen them up to about 1 000 pounds in size; however, from the literature we know they can get up to 3 000 pounds or more. I had never seen juveniles or 'baby' ocean sunfishes before the summer of 1996, when we started seeing these little 2- to 3-pound, dinnerplate size, juveniles off the coast of San Diego, California. The little sunfishes always appeared in tight schools of 5 to 30 or more individuals."
Richard Herrmann.

Atlantic puffins. Vestmannaeyjar, Iceland. © **Frans Lanting**

Tufted puffin. Farallon Islands, California, USA. © **Kevin Schafer**

This is perhaps the most popular of all seabirds. Puffins are often mistaken for penguins, but in fact they are not related to them at all. However, although they live on opposite poles, they share similar adaptations to the cold marine environment, such as two-tone coloration and compact bodies.

"I began my career as a seabird biologist, studying the birds of the Farallon Islands, just thirty miles away from San Francisco, California. Many thousands of birds nested here, but my favorites were always the tufted puffins. Perhaps it is their colorful beaks, or their stylish head plumes, but they have always seemed to have the most personality of any birds except penguins. This puffin had a nest burrow very close to our research blind, and I was able to watch it coming and going every day." Kevin Schafer.

Pacific white-sided dolphin. Northwest Pacific Ocean. © **F. Stuart Westmorland**

This species can form groups of up to thousands of individuals of all ages and both sexes. Apparently, they also seek the company of other marine mammals such as the northern right-whale dolphin; the distribution of these two species is practically identical.

Sperm whale tail. New Zealand. © **Flip Nicklin**/Minden Pictures

"Whales, majestic creatures of the seas, with whom we share this planet, are among the largest to ever have existed, and descend into worlds that most of us will never know." Patricio Robles Gil.

Orangefin anemonefish. Red Sea.
© **Mike Bacon**

Clown anemonefishes. Papua New Guinea.
© **Mike Bacon**

"Swimming along a soft coral encrusted wall, I discovered a quite large anemone home to a single orangefin anemonefish. I marveled at the curious nature of the clown fish within this unusually red anemone allowing for wonderful close focus opportunities much to my delight." Mike Bacon.

"These flamboyantly-colored anemonefishes among the tentacles of the rare purple color phase of the anemone was a combination that could not be passed by. This anemone was host to a semipermanent monogamous pair of adult fishes and several small juveniles." Mike Bacon.

Humpback whale and calf. Tonga, Polynesia.
© **Jean-Marc La Roque**/Auscape

Icebergs caught in frozen ice shelf. Weddell Sea, Antarctica.
© **Konrad Wothe**/ENP Images

"Whales in mid-ocean, suspended in the waves of the sea / great heaven of whales in the waters, old hierarchies. / And enormous mother whales lie dreaming / suckling their whale eyes wide open / in the waters of the beginning and the end." D. H. Lawrence.

"The wild places are where we began. When they end, so do we."
David Brower.

Black-browed albatross in storm. Subantarctica.
© **Frans Lanting**/Minden Pictures

With the exception of four species, the distribution of albatrosses is limited to the southern hemisphere, where this bird family evolved. Albatrosses spend most of the time in the air traversing great distances, since their perfect design allows them to remain in flight with a minimum of effort, as if they enjoyed blizzards and storms.

Brant geese. Guerrero Negro Lagoon, Baja California, Mexico.
© **Patricio Robles Gil**/Sierra Madre

Estuaries are very important for many species throughout the world, since they constitute areas for feeding, nesting, and wintering for millions of water birds such as herons, ducks, and Brant geese. Ninety percent of world fishing activities is conducted in coastal regions; of this figure, 70% involves organisms that spend most of their lives in a lagoon ecosystem.

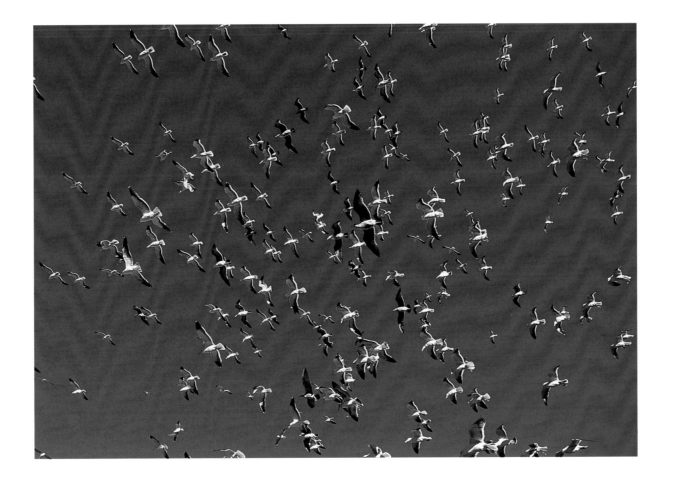

Galápagos penguins. Galápagos Islands, Ecuador.
© **D. Parer** & **E. Parer-Cook**/Auscape

Surrounded by anchovies, the figure of a penguin stands out against the sea. The diversity of marine life on and around the Galápagos Islands has caused the admiration of many scientists, including Darwin in the mid-nineteenth century.

Seagulls. Cedros Island, Baja California, Mexico.
© **Patricio Robles Gil**/Sierra Madre

Framed by the blue of the sky, hundreds of seagulls patrol the beaches and coasts. They leave the place where they were born and winter in more tropical areas. The northern hemisphere contains the greatest diversity of these seabirds.

Walruses. Round Island, Alaska, USA.
© **Art Wolfe**

On the beaches, walruses come together forming living textures. When they emerge from the water, their white bodies become rose-colored to prevent hyperthermia. If their temperature rises too much, walruses have to roll to the sea in order to cool themselves down.

Group of narwhals. Baffin Island, Canada.
© **Flip Nicklin**/Minden Pictures

"Thus, so long as more concrete statements do not exist, I abide by the opinion that this is a marine unicorn of supernatural dimensions armed, not with a halberd, but with a kind of ram, like battleships, and with an equal amount of motive power." Jules Verne.

Adélie penguins. Hope Bay, Antarctic Peninsula.
© **Patricio Robles Gil**/Sierra Madre

On this small iceberg, a group of penguins has found a base for planning their arrival on land. Fearing the appearance of some predator, they look around nervously in all directions. Any movement may cause alarm among them, even the approach of a new companion.

Adélie penguins. Hope Bay, Antarctic Peninsula.
© **Patricio Robles Gil**/Sierra Madre

"Although it is small, the dramatic expression on its face distinguishes it greatly from the other penguins. The white ring around the eyes makes them so expressive that you can perceive their fear when they hurl themselves into the sea, since that is when their main predator, the leopard seal, catches them. So as to confuse it, penguins gather together at the edges and jump in one after the other en masse."
Patricio Robles Gil.

Yellow-footed gull. Gulf of California, Mexico.
© **Fulvio Eccardi**

Heermann's gulls. Rasa Island, Gulf of California, Mexico.
© **Fulvio Eccardi**

"The sea is measured by waves / the sky, by wings / and we humans, by tears."
Jaime Sabines.

"At times, weather conditions are critical in a nesting colony of seabirds. In 1986, when this photo was taken, strong, constant winds prevented adult Heermann's gulls from going out to sea in search of food, and the weakest of the terns' chicks were easy prey to these hungry, opportunistic birds." Fulvio Eccardi.

Bearded seal. Norway.

© **Flip Nicklin**/Minden Pictures

Humpback whale. Kona Island, Hawaii, USA.

© **Christopher Newbert**

This seal is characterized by the bright color of its face, which it gets from the iron that is found in the soils where it feeds; another of its peculiarities is the song it emits underwater, which can be heard many kilometers away. This song, as well as its bubbling, are considered courtship rituals to attract the female.

"Animals are nothing but the forms of our virtues and vices, wandering before our eyes, the visible phantoms of our souls." Victor Hugo.

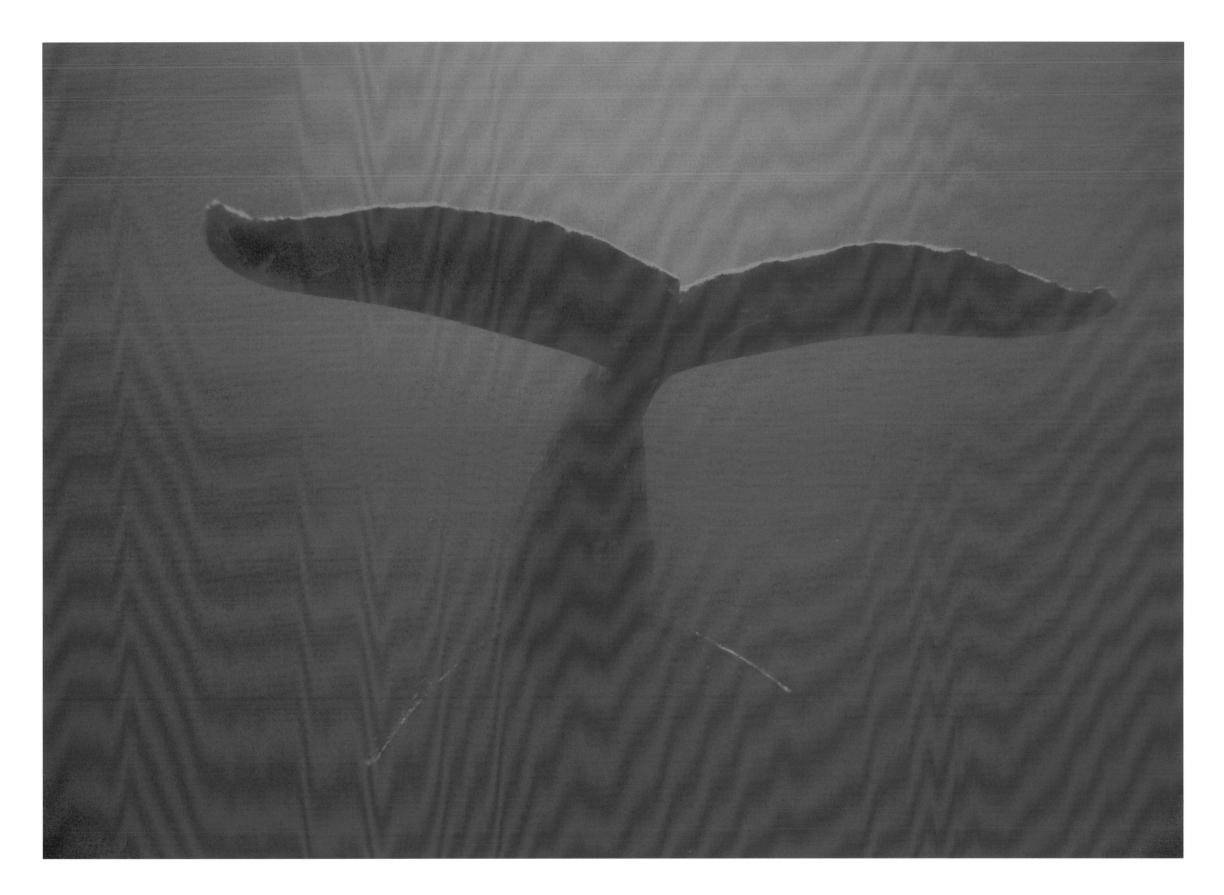

Glover reef in Caribbean Sea. Belize.
© **Kenneth Garrett**/National Geographic Society

"And so the clouds that filled the space between the sky and the earth opened up. Under them and over the water on the surface there began to appear the hills and mountains that can be seen today." *Popol Vuh*.

Eye of bluechin parrot fish. Clipperton Island, France.
© **Richard Herrmann**

"We went to the sea. [...] It seemed as if it were looking at us from within, from deep down, with many eyes, with eyes just like the ones we have in our hearts to see at a distance or in the dark." Jaime Sabines.

Caribbean spiny lobsters. Bahama Islands.
© **Howard Hall**/Howard Hall Productions

Green sea turtle. Los Roques Islands, Venezuela.
© **F. Stuart Westmorland**

The photographer comments that he shot this picture of Caribbean spiny lobsters in the Bahamas while they were migrating from the shallow waters of the sand banks to the deeper waters of the reefs after the first storm of the season.

After they are born, male sea turtles never return to land; they live forever in the sea and only approach the coasts to mate. A very smallpercentage of sea turtles reach adulthood.

King penguin with chick. South Georgia Island, UK.
© **Patricio Robles Gil**/Sierra Madre

Black-footed albatrosses. Midway Atoll, Hawaii, USA.
© **Kevin Schafer**

Unlike some reptiles and fishes, for birds parenthood is an exhausting chore that lasts weeks or, in the case of this king penguin, over a year. During that time, the male has shared with the female the responsibility for feeding their chick; however, today's menu doesn't seem to be very appealing to this little one.

"I spent ten days on Midway Atoll in the mid-Pacific, photographing the enormous numbers of nesting seabirds that cover almost every inch of the island. Once the site of a major U.S. military base, and the center of the most important naval battle of World War II, Midway has now become a refuge for wildlife. With no predators, these black-footed albatrosses nest directly on the sand and are unafraid of humans, despite the fact that they have a very small chick." Kevin Schafer.

Galápagos shark. Galápagos Islands, Ecuador.
© **Christopher Newbert**

Caribbean reef shark. Caribbean Sea.
© **Tom Campbell**

"We are kin to the stars, members of a universal family. The sea is part of that connection. It is a visual poem celebrating not just the intrincate fabric of life which evolution has woven here, but the origin and life force common to all things." Christopher Newbert.

The fishermen of the world catch between 30 and 100 million sharks every year. Often only their fins are used to make soup; the fins are cut off of live sharks which are then released back into the ocean, completely helpless and unable to move, for which reason they die of asphyxiation shortly thereafter.

Pages 136-137
Cactus forest. Cholludo Island, Gulf of California, Mexico.
© **George H. H. Huey**

On the Gulf of California, one of the richest on this planet, there are over 50 islands whose geological origins and distance from the coast differ, for which reason each is home to endemic plants and animals. Many of these are Cactaceae, which give these islands their unique appearance.

Kelp gull. Livingston Island, Antarctic Peninsula.
© **Patricio Robles Gil**/Sierra Madre

"Like the sea itself, seabirds are enigmatic. We know very little about them, since all of them must return to land to breed and it is there where we study them. As they go further out to sea, our knowledge of them becomes more and more limited, leaving us somewhere between fascination and mystery." Patricio Robles Gil.

Gray whale. Magdalena Bay, Baja California Sur, Mexico.
© **François Gohier**

One of the most beautiful phenomena in the marine realm is repeated year after year on the coastal lagoons of Baja California, when gray whales arrive there and breed. Theirs is a conservation success story; they are now out of danger, numbering over 20 thousand individuals. When their calves come close and humans get a chance to admire them and touch them with great emotion, we do not know who is the more curious of the two.

Harbor seal in giant kelp. Cannery Row, California, USA.
© **Chuck Davis**

Stingrays. Grand Cayman Island, UK.
© **James D. Watt**/Innerspace Visions

These spectacular clusters of marine algae grow near the coast and in temperate seas. They are like underwater forests, where kelp looks like trees, and the fishes and marine mammals look like birds.

A very common scene in these waters is to see stingrays in the shallows, either buried in the sand or looking for food, which they never see because their eyes are on the top of their head and their mouth, in the lower part. Nevertheless, their other senses, which are very keen, enable them to locate their food.

Black-browed albatrosses. Falkland Islands, UK.
© **Patricio Robles Gil**/Sierra Madre

Most albatrosses conduct complex courting rituals before they mate. These rituals reaffirm the union of couples, which usually remain together for life.

King penguins. Falkland Islands, UK.
© **Wayne Lynch**

Among penguins, 60 to 90% of the females select the same mate as the year before. However, this can vary greatly in the larger species due to the difficulties that arise in their reproductive cycles. One example of this are king penguins: only a third are faithful to their mates.

Leafy sea dragon. Australia.
© **Norbert Wu**

On rare occasions, the leafy sea dragon allows us to observe its singular beauty. Most of the time it is hidden, blending in with its environment. Yet its appearance is brief, because its survival depends on its being able to go unnoticed in the proximity of numerous predators that share its habitat.

Napoleon wrasse. Red Sea.
© **Mike Bacon**

This wrasse, which can reach a weight of over 200 kg and a length of 2 m, is extremely curious, exploring everything that happens around it. The large prominence on its head is a distinguishing feature of adult males, a characteristic that is shared with other species such as parrot fishes.

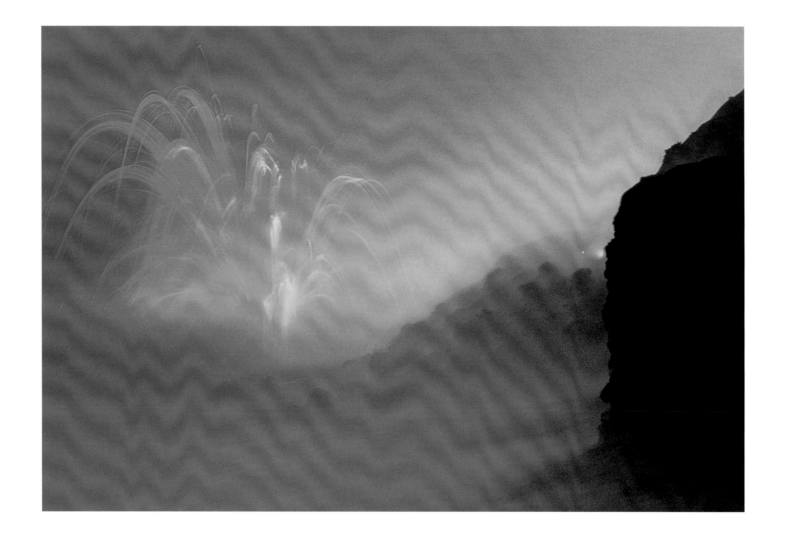

Lava. Hawaii, USA.
© **Art Wolfe**

A lovely incandescent fountain spills its liquid magma into the sea. Many landscapes and seascapes have been formed through volcanic activity, which emerges from the heart of our planet.

Wager Bay. Northwest Territories, Canada.
© **Thomas D. Mangelsen**

"And I / ask you for nothing, nothing / that comes from the other world: / only / the light on the sea, / the barefoot light on the sleeping land and sea." Octavio Paz.

Pink squat lobster. Great Barrier Reef, Australia.
© **Roger Steene**/ENP Images

Clown fish in sea anemone. Indonesia.
© **Marylou McCray**

In the underwater world, many invertebrates make themselves virtually invisible to their predators, just like insects do in jungles. The struggle for survival among these small creatures is as unrelenting as in any other natural setting.

Sea anemones are dangerously toxic for the majority of the fishes that live in the same habitat. Only clown fishes are immune to sea anemones, a fact that they take advantage of, seeking refuge in them and thus escaping from their predators.

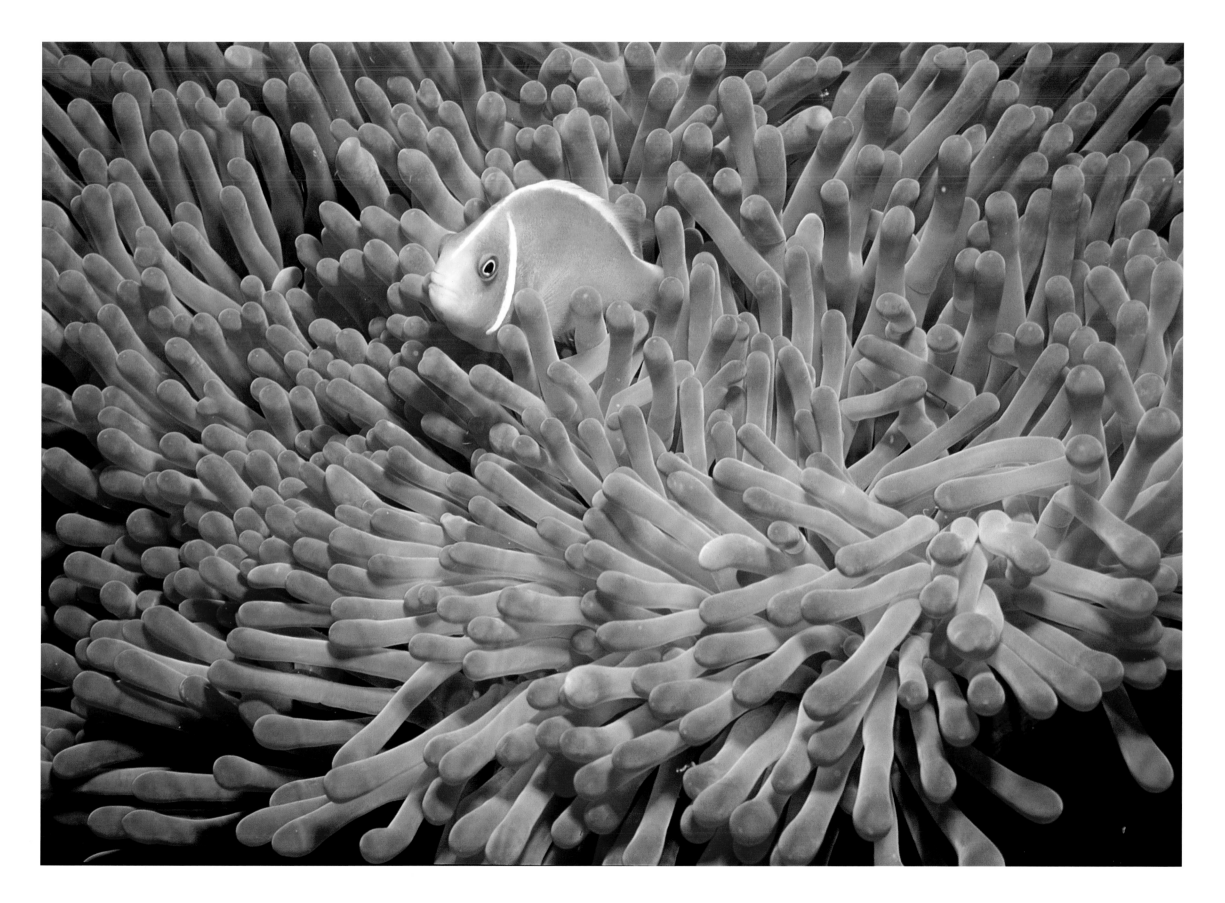

Humpback whale. Northern Pacific Ocean.
© **Brandon D. Cole**/ENP Images

Polar bear. Baffin Island, Canada.
© **Flip Nicklin**/Minden Pictures

The interplay of differences is what keeps the world going. Life is always plural, while death makes everything uniform.

The "bear of the frozen seas" is the largest carnivorous mammal, and one of the few mammals with amphibious capabilities. It evolved from an exclusively terrestrial ancestor, before the last glaciation. One of its adaptations to the marine environment is the length of its neck, which allows it to maintain its head above the water while swimming.

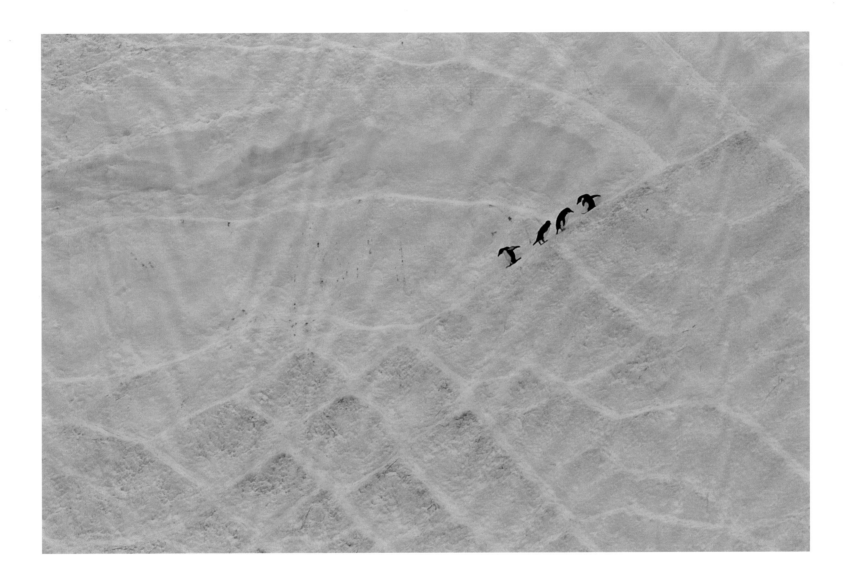

King penguins. South Georgia Island, UK.
© **Patricio Robles Gil**/Sierra Madre

Macaroni penguins. South Georgia Island, UK.
© **Patricio Robles Gil**/Sierra Madre

"I had the opportunity to spend an entire day amidst this colony of king penguins. I couldn't help feeling amazed at the sight: anywhere I looked, I could see thousands of penguins forming extraordinary patterns. At the same time, I thought about how hard it would be, in this colony, to be a parent and have to find my child by trumpeting in the middle of a concert played by 50 thousand trumpets." Patricio Robles Gil.

"On the nearly 30-meter high wall of ice they carved some very narrow paths, and when two groups of penguins met face to face, they were courteous to an extreme. Two days earlier, I saw a penguin fall from a height of over 10 meters, bounce against the ice, and continue on its way." Patricio Robles Gil.

Spotted anemone crabs living on a magnificent sea anemone.
Bali, Indonesia. © **Fred Bavendam**/Minden Pictures

Emperor shrimp on sea cucumber. Indonesia.
© **Burt Jones**/**Maurine Shimlock**/Secret Sea

Like clown fishes, these two crabs take refuge in the protective cover of their host, waiting for some distracted fish to fall into its tentacles so they can eat as much of it as they can, while it is taken little by little into the great mouth of the sea anemone.

Sliding along the entire length of the spotted body of this sea cucumber, this small shrimp —like others of its close relatives that live on the underside of some sea stars— spends its whole life associated with these animals, which move very slowly, mainly because they lack the sufficient strength to keep up with faster swimmers.

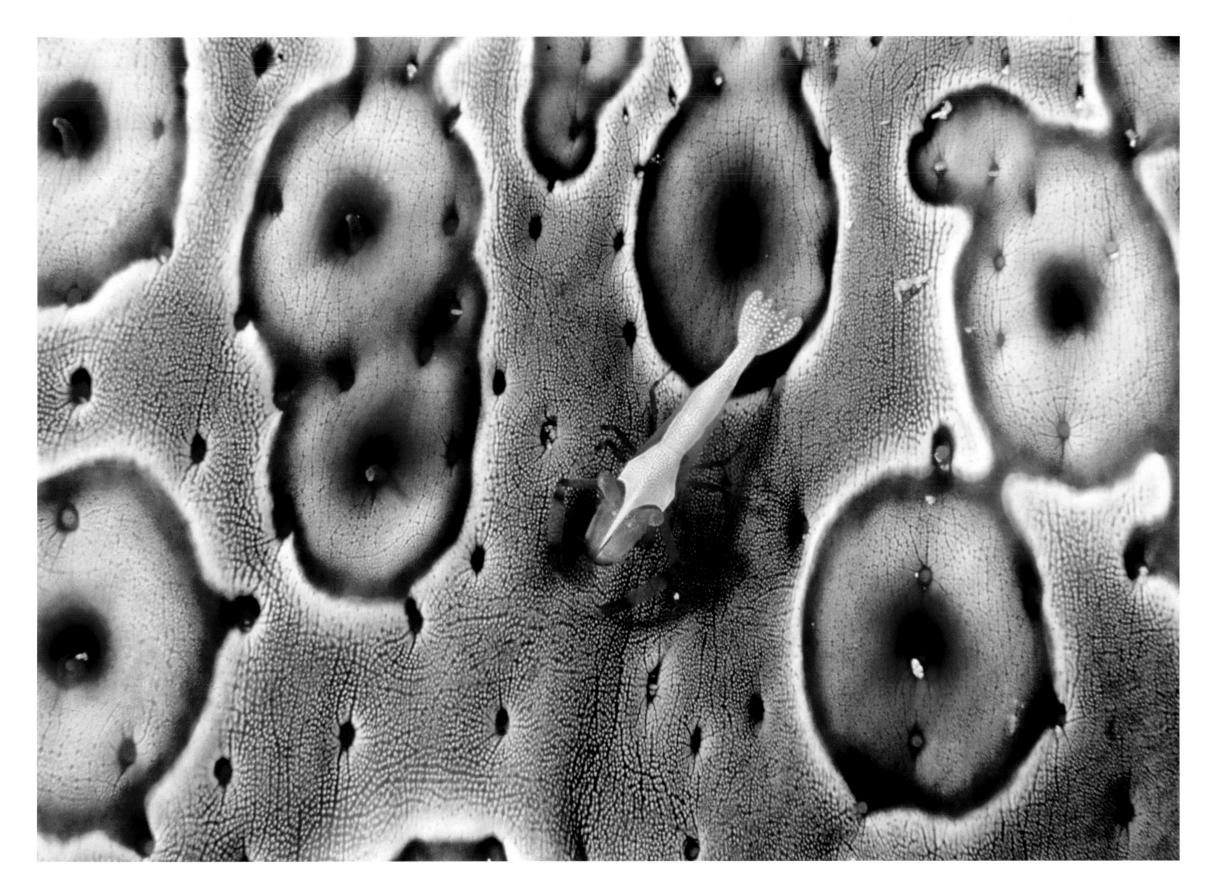

California sea otter. Monterey Bay, California, USA.
© **Jeff Foott**

Southern elephant seals. Fortuna Bay, South Georgia Island, UK.
© **Patricio Robles Gil**/Sierra Madre

The gesticulations and expressions of sea otters are very similar to those of human beings, and that is why we find them so appealing. Jeff Foott was able to capture this, and has received wide recognition for this photo, as well as for the book and documentary he prepared on this species.

"On land, elephant seals are like enormous bags of potatoes stretched out, carefree, on the beach. For example, it took this pup over an hour to get rid of this weight." Patricio Robles Gil.

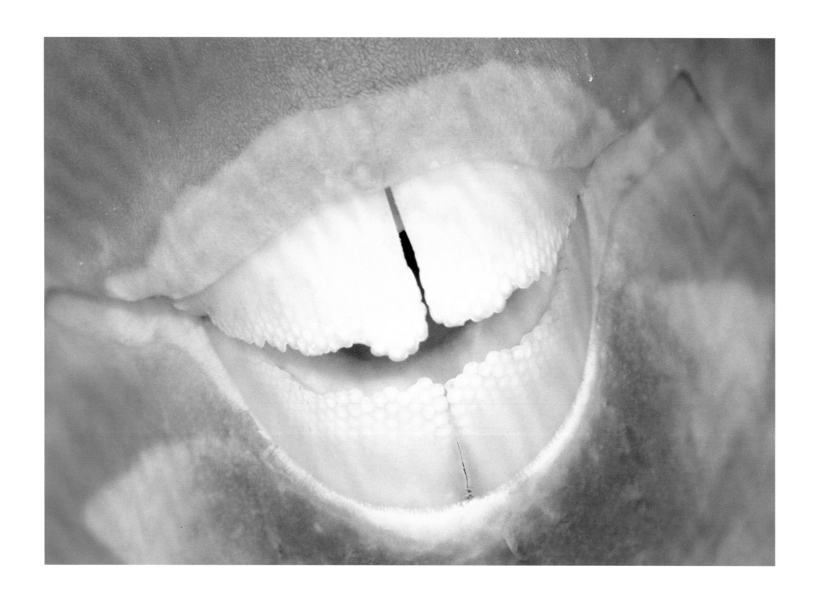

Mouth of parrot fish. Red Sea © **Christopher Newbert**

"Its name suits it well. The teeth of the parrot fish have been fused into a parrot-like beak. The rich green and blue coloration of these fishes is reminiscent of a parrot's feathers." Christopher Newbert.

Fin of parrot fish. Red Sea © **Christopher Newbert**

"Parrot fishes quite literally fly through the water on gossamer wings. Their pectoral fins, so delicate and sheer, are their primary means of locomotion. Only when frightened will they use their more powerful tail fins." Christopher Newbert.

Great white shark. Neptune Islands, Australia.
© **Chuck Davis**

Blue rockfish. Kelp forest, California, USA.
© **Brandon D. Cole**/ENP Images

"After spending hundreds of hours in the water with the great white shark, I can say that there's a lot more to their behavior and personality than just razor-sharp teeth and bloody water. I've seen great whites as beautiful, finely-tuned oceanic creatures." Chuck Davis.

Kelp forests grow in the depths like exuberant rain forests do on land. The diversity of species of this extraordinary marine habitat is also very large; a great variety of fishes, mollusks, crustaceans, and marine mammals such as seals and otters, are some of the 800 species that live in different levels of the kelp forest.

Polar bear and cubs. Northwest Territories, Canada.
© Art Wolfe

Polar bear and cubs. Wapusk National Park, Manitoba, Canada.
© Thomas D. Mangelsen

Polar bears have adapted extraordinarily well to life in the Arctic. Their fur is so thick that very little water reaches their skin. The females usually have two cubs in the winter, which remain with their mother for nearly two years, following her very closely, even in the sea.

Brunnich's guillemot. Cape Fanshawe, Norwegian Arctic.
© **Tui De Roy**/The Roving Tortoise

Cormorants and rainbow. Australia.
© **David Doubilet**

The majority of seabirds are distributed along the coasts. For ages, they have nested on remote islands, isolated for hundreds of miles around. In these nesting sites are found different topographies and habitats. Some colonies of birds form on cliffs; others group together on the flat areas of deserted islands beyond the reach of terrestrial predators. The pollution of the seas and overfishing are reducing bird colonies throughout the world.

Lion-fish juvenile. Suruga Bay, Japan.
© David Doubilet

"This is the most jewel-like, exquisite fish I'd ever seen, the size of a silver dollar, fluttering like a butterfly. I approached it with care because for all its delicacy its venomous spines appeared to be in perfect working order." David Doubilet, *Ocean Realm.*

Moray eel and orange coral. Izu Bay, Japan.
© David Doubilet

Hunters by night, moray eels come out in the open when the sun begins to set, in search of food, slithering along the corals near their refuges, to which they often return to eat their prey or to hide, if necessary, to avoid being captured by one of their predators.

Two-spot gobies. Solomon Islands.
© **Christopher Newbert**

"Typically found in pairs in sandy areas, these fishes quickly dive into the holes that they dig if they are disturbed, or use the two large spots on their fins as a 'predator mimic' coloration pattern to protect themselves." Christopher Newbert.

Mantis shrimp. Solomon Islands.
© **Christopher Newbert**

Motionless, the mantis shrimp lays in wait for some prey, hoping to go unnoticed; once it has its prey within its reach, it will trap it at lightning speed, in a movement that is among the quickest in the animal kingdom.

Whale shark. Kona Island, Hawaii, USA.

© **James D. Watt**/Innerspace Visions

This enormous fish, the biggest of all, is an extremely gentle creature which seems to enjoy the company of humans.

Pacific green sea turtle. Coronado Island, Southern California, USA.

© **Mike Johnson**

"Rare in these temperate waters, perhaps propelled northward by warmer than usual currents in an 'El Niño' year, this lone animal was found resting in the summer sun while juvenile jack mackerel sought the shelter of its shadow." Mike Johnson.

Aerial view. Sinai, Egypt.
© **David Doubilet**

"A meeting place for Africa and Asia [...] relatively young as
seas go, it was born as a crack in the desert floor 25 million
years ago. The sea floor continues to widen by about an
inch a year. No river flows into this desert sea. [...] The sea
sits isolated amid these desolate lands like a mammoth
aquarium." David Doubilet, National Geographic Society.

Mountains, mist, and iceberg. Le Maire Strait, Antarctica.
© **Joseph Van Os**

"Nature gives to every time and season some beauties of its
own; and from morning to night, as from the cradle to the
grave, is but a succession of changes so gentle and easy
that we can scarcely mark their progress."
Charles Dickens.

Antarctic fur seal pups. South Georgia Island, UK.
© **Patricio Robles Gil**/Sierra Madre

Orca and sea lion pup. Argentina.
© **Jasmine Rossi**/Innerspace Visions

The population of fur seals on South Georgia Island was discovered at the close of the eighteenth century, and soon afterwards thirty English and Russian ships exploited the skins of the fur seal population until this animal became extinct. In 1933 a small population of them was found on Bird Island, north of South Georgia. Thanks to protective legislation, this population now numbers over two million.

In the face of the orca's enormous display of strength when it attacks, even outside the water there is no guarantee of safety. The ability of these cetaceans to turn over icebergs where there are seals or penguins and prey upon them in the water has been documented.

Emperor penguin. Antarctica. © **Hans Reinhard**/Bruce Coleman Ltd.

"Exploding through a hole in the ice, an emperor rockets from the sea. Graceless on land, emperors are Olympian swimmers, capable of diving to 1 750 feet to hunt fish. To elude leopard seals that lurk at the ice's edge, they accelerate as they near the surface, leaving contrails of air bubbles in their wakes and catapulting as high as seven feet out of the water." Glenn Oeland, National Geographic Society.

Steller sea eagle. Hokkaido, Japan. © Orion Service & Trading Co. Inc./Bruce Coleman Ltd.

"The eagles strike the limitless space, the fishes glide in the shallows; under a frosty sky, all the creatures compete in freedom." Mao Tse-Tung.

Hammerhead sharks. Galápagos Islands, Ecuador.
© **Christopher Newbert**

Hammerhead sharks group together at certain times of the year, following an order dictated by millions of years of evolution, in relatively small areas and for periods of several weeks. Their groups, numbering as many as several hundred, are so orderly that they are known as "schools."

Atlantic spotted dolphins. Bahama Islands.
© **Doug Perrine**/Innerspace Visions

It was completely calm, the sun was at its peak, the image of the dolphins was so perfect, that for seconds it was impossible to tell which was real and which was the reflection.

Antarctic mountains. Le Maire Strait, Antarctic Peninsula.
© **Winland Smith**/Jeff Foott Productions

Humpback whales. Alaska, USA.
© **Brandon D. Cole**/Innerspace Visions

"Dominated solely by ice, the Antarctic offers humankind the opportunity to conserve the last natural refuge. The challenge of our generation is to leave an example in which our interest is peace and cooperation in a common territory for all humans." Georgina Ferrer.

"Amidst a whirlwind of water and fishes, they emerge as majestic mountains; the great feast, the age-old ritual that takes place every summer." Patricio Robles Gil.

Mustard rays. Galápagos Islands, Ecuador.
© **Birgitte Wilms**

"As soon as we entered the water, we were lucky to encounter this school of rays. They were kind enough to make several passes, and as they swam over us, they left me with an unforgettable image of ten smiling faces." Birgitte Wilms.

Napoleon fish. Red Sea.
© **Christopher Newbert**

"I have many times had the sense of being watched. Turning quickly, I have often been greeted by what seems to be nothing but a huge, rotating eyeball with a really massive fish attached." Christopher Newbert.

"[...] crawling together on flat tables of rock or letting themselves drop into the sea with loud reports I beheld huge
slimy monsters —soft snails, as it were, of incredible
bigness— two or three score of them together, making the
rocks to echo with their barkings." R. L. Stevenson.

Orcas are mistakenly known as killer whales, although in
fact they belong to the dolphin family. In the past they
were considered a dangerous competitor for fishermen;
however, today they are regarded with affection.

"These sea lions followed me around for most of the dive.
Perhaps they were fascinated by their own reflections in
the dome port of my underwater camera housing and then
dispersed just to begin another dive-bombing raid."
Chuck Davis.

Royal tern. Tulum, Quintana Roo, Mexico.
© **Claudio Contreras**

Gannets. Scotland, UK.
© **Mike Cruise**

"Near the water, on the water, one learns to sail over the clouds, to swim in the heavens." Gaston Bachelard.

"Suspended in a blue sky, time seems to stand still until the rising wind declines and breaks the spell, obliging hundreds of birds to return to their nests or to flap their wings and continue their flight in an endless search for food." Pablo Cervantes.

Orcas. Solomon Islands.
© **Birgitte Wilms**

Family groups of common orcas join together for life, even as many as four generations of them. They move in pods which are most feared, and for this reason have been called "wolves of the sea."

Sperm whale. North Atlantic Ocean.
© **François Gohier**/Auscape

"Sperm whales live most of their lives deep in the seas, foraging in a habitat of great pressure and almost total darkness, an environment we understand less well than we understand the surface of the moon." Hal Whitehead, National Geographic Society.

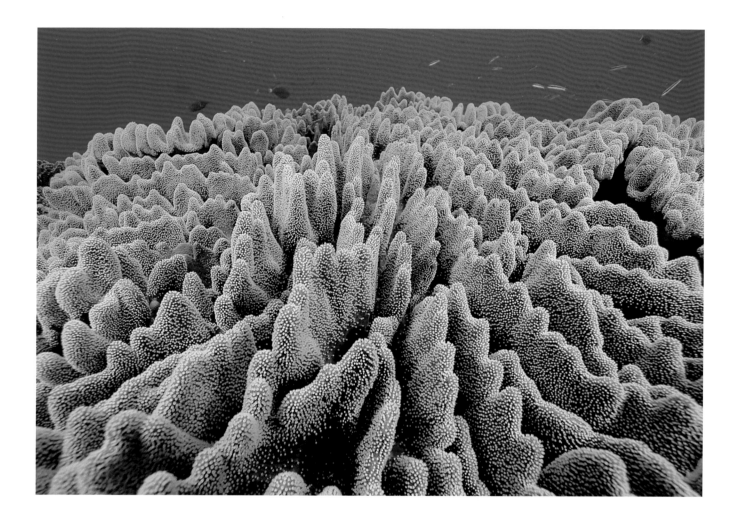

Leather coral. Solomon Islands.
© **Christopher Newbert**

Galápagos shark. Galápagos Islands, Ecuador.
© **Birgitte Wilms**

"These corals exist in a wide variety of species. This one forms extensive lush carpets covering the reef. Its low profile and leathery flexibility mean they are resilient to strong currents and heavy surges from storm waves." Christopher Newbert.

"The brawny Galápagos shark wove in and out of the shallow water, as if playing hide and seek. They seem to avoid eye contact, often approaching divers from behind. Every once in a while they become curious or bold, moving in for a closer look." Birgitte Wilms.

Inca terns. San Gallán Island, Paracas, Peru.
© **Patricio Robles Gil**/Sierra Madre

Arctic terns. Canadian Arctic.
© **Norbert Rosing**/Animals Animals

The cold Humboldt Current bathes the southwestern coast of South America as far as Peru, enriching its waters with nutrients. Diverse species take advantage of this phenomenon. Outstanding among them is the emblematic Inca tern, exclusive to this zone.

It has been said that the Arctic tern can resist flights longer than the Earth's circumference, since it makes the lengthiest migration known in the animal world. This seabird travels 35 thousand kilometers from pole to pole, and then sets off on its return journey. In the photograph, a male is courting a female, offering her food.

Twelve Apostles. Port Campbell National Park, Australia.
© **Art Wolfe**

Ojo de Liebre Lagoon. Baja California Sur, Mexico.
© **Patricio Robles Gil**/Sierra Madre

"Few people realize that water is, in one way, the strongest thing on Earth."
Christopher N. Palmer.

"The sun was hidden behind the mountains. Perhaps they were also contemplating the sunset, always toward the west, under the deep cloak of the sea. The light faded and the sky took on a rainbow of colors. Only the silhouettes eluded those colors." Patricio Robles Gil.

Soft coral. Solomon Islands.
© **Christopher Newbert**

Lion-fish. Red Sea.
© **Christopher Newbert**

"No single picture can truly do justice to the grandeur of this undersea garden. The fact that in many cases we have been the first human eyes to embrace these marine vistas is humbling." Christopher Newbert.

"Soaring regally above me on a color-splashed red sea reef, a lion-fish fans its elegant fins into the current. The nonaggressive nature of this fish makes them a delight to observe and photograph without any threat of harm." Christopher Newbert.

Gentoo penguin. Antarctic Peninsula.

© **Patricio Robles Gil**/Sierra Madre

Royal penguins. Macquarie Island, Australia.

© **Tui De Roy**/The Roving Tortoise

Penguins are a symbol of the Antarctic. Although the seventeen species are only found in the southern hemisphere, most occur above the Antarctic Circle. In fact, one of these is located at the equator, on the Galápagos Islands. Penguins are the most aquatic of seabirds, and although they have totally lost their ability to fly, under the water they "fly" most swiftly.

Bullock's chromodorid nudibranchs. Bali, Indonesia.
© **Fred Bavendam**/Minden Pictures

Life on our planet is a fragile web in which all of its creatures interact in a delicate balance. None, however insignificant or unattractive they may seem to us, can be overlooked.

Anemonefish on sea anemone. Solomon Islands.
© **Michele B. Hall**/Howard Hall Productions

A clown fish hides from the photographer in the safety of a sea anemone, and will not come out until she has retreated far enough away and it no longer feels threatened.

Falesia Beach. Portugal.
© **Candy Lopesino** & **Juan Hidalgo**

"Roll on, thou deep and dark blue Ocean—roll! / [...] Man marks the earth with ruin—his control / Stops with the shore." Lord Byron.

Rainbow and storm. Australia.
© **Mitsuaki Iwago**/Minden Pictures

"...although it is believed or is proven that the world is of a round figure like a ball, not for that reason can it be affirmed that in that other part of the world the land is uncovered and without water." Joseph de Acosta.

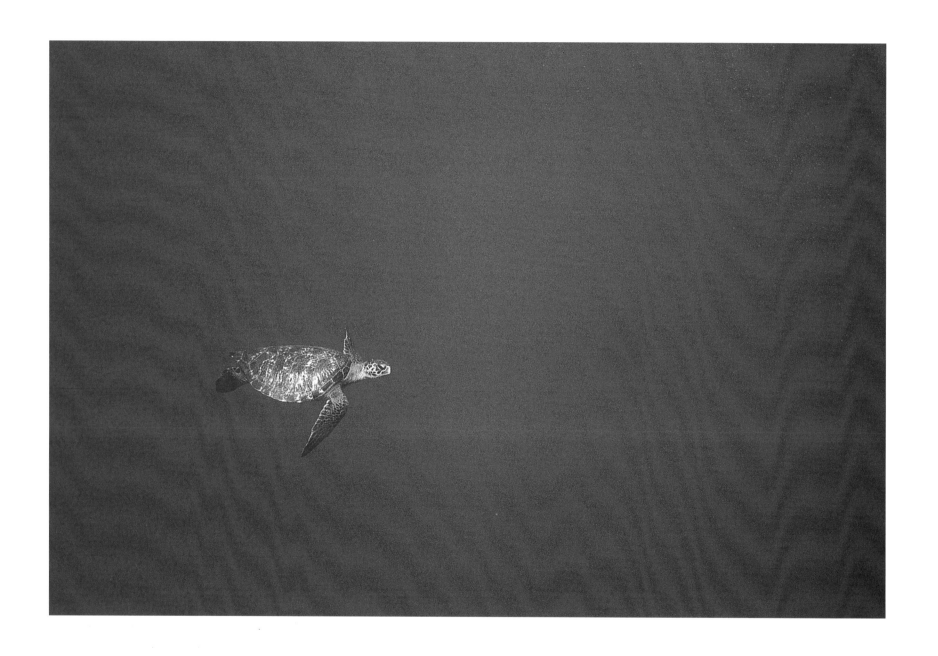

Green sea turtle. The Seamount, Gulf of California, Mexico. © **Pablo Cervantes**/Sierra Madre

"After a long dive, I made a decompression stop, surrounded only by the deep blue of the sea. Suddenly, out of nowhere appeared a turtle, keeping me company as if it understood how strange its aquatic habitat was for me." Pablo Cervantes.

Caribbean reef shark. Quitasueño Key, Colombia. © **Aldo Brando**

"With an imposing presence, the king of the deep suddenly appears in the front yard of its domain. This shark, two meters of muscle and cartilage, approaches the surface above the Elkhorn corals." Aldo Brando.

Starfishes. Olympic Peninsula, Washington, USA.
© **Jack Dykinga**

The tide rises and falls since time immemorial, intermittently uncovering many coastal species such as these starfishes, which have adapted to surviving under changing air and water conditions.

Western gull. California, USA.
© **Richard Herrmann**

"The central California coast has a very diverse and colorful assemblage of marine algae species. The best time to see these spectacular marine plants is at minus tide. In this image, a western gull sits on an exposed rock during a minus tide at the Montaña de Oro State Park."
Richard Herrmann.

Australian sea lion. Neptune Islands, Australia.
© **Howard Hall**/Howard Hall Productions

Guillemots. Arctic.
© **Doug Allan**/Oxford Scientific Films

"We have played god with the planet and the lives of its creatures. Their ultimate fate is our responsibility. It is also our destiny." Bill Yeates.

These birds seem to be cut out for swimming, rather than for flying. When they dive in search of food, they propel themselves forward with their wings in a swift aquatic "flight" that leaves an unmistakable trail of bubbles. They can remain under water for almost two minutes, and reach depths of up to 9 meters.

Cape Flattery. Washington, USA.
© **Art Wolfe**

"In late afternoons at sea, the gradual arrival of night and the retreating light draw on the water and sky a world of chromatic geographies that are unique, fleeting, and always new." Blanca Luz Pulido.

Second Beach. Olympic Peninsula, Washington, USA.
© **Jack Dykinga**

"The mirror-like surface of the receding waves began to reflect the crimson clouds of sunset. I just decided to forget about the rising tide and concentrate on the circular pond around the rock in the foreground. I got wet... and this photograph, too!" Jack Dykinga.

Short-finned pilot whales. Kona Island, Hawaii, USA. © 1989. **Bob Talbot**/Talbot Productions

Highly gregarious, these cetaceans form groups of up to hundreds of individuals that move together to avoid interfering with each other's sonar. At times
they can be seen resting placidly on the surface for several hours, practically motionless, although they are watching out for any possible danger.

Lion and skeleton of pilot whale. Coast of Namibia. © **Des** & **Jen Bartlett**/National Geographic Society

"Where desert and ocean collide in a land of the unexpected, a lion feasts on a pilot whale stranded on Namibia's desolate shore."
Des & Jen Bartlett.

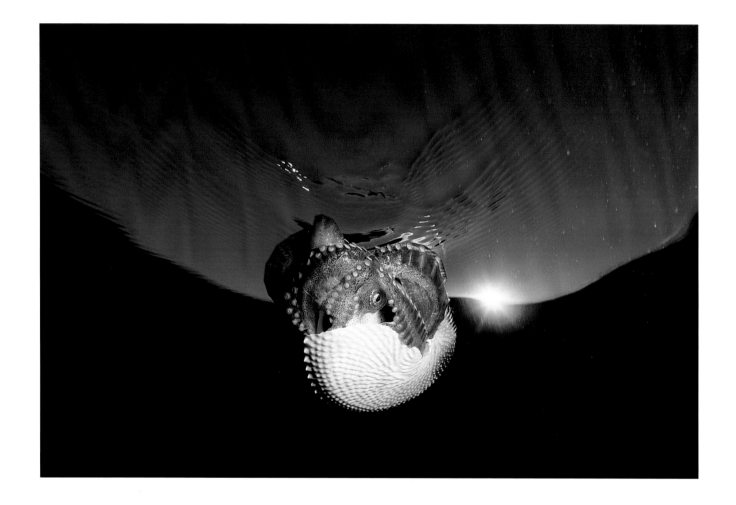

Paper nautilus. Port Phillip Bay, Australia.
© **D. Parer** & **E. Parer-Cook**/Auscape

The elegant shell of this mollusk, which rises from the depths in the late afternoon to feed, is found only in the female. It fulfills two important functions: to protect the eggs females deposit in it while they are developing, and as a refuge for the delicate, smaller male, which seeks shelter inside the shell when it senses danger.

Fairy tern. Hawaii, USA.
© **Frans Lanting**

"He was sorry for the birds, especially the small delicate dark terns that were always flying and looking and almost never finding."
Ernest Hemingway.

Cape Flattery. Washington, USA.
© **Kevin Schafer**

Fin whale. Gulf of California, Mexico.
© **François Gohier**

"The northwest corner of the United States is a dramatic meeting of land and sea, often shrouded in mist and fog. The sounds here are vivid: the restless crashing of the surf on the sandstone cliffs, and the plaintive cries of seabirds, like these glaucous-winged gulls. Although I travel all over the world, this will always be one of my favorite places." Kevin Schafer.

"To float like the soul of life, to depart like a voice, / to experience this moment tremulously on eternal waters." Fernando Pessoa.

Walruses. Cape Pearce, Alaska, USA.
© Art Wolfe

Walruses. Ellesmere Island, Northwest Territories, Canada.
© Thomas D. Mangelsen

Walruses are undoubtedly one of the strangest animals on Earth: they have an amorphous, stocky body and a small head flanked by two long tusks. In fact, the length of their tusks is what gives the males certain status in territorial disputes. They are found in waters near the coast and rest on large blocks of ice.

Garden eels. Red Sea.
© **David Doubilet**

School of squid. Suruga Bay, Japan.
© **David Doubilet**

The photographer took this picture with a remote-controlled camera, after the three weeks that it took the eels to get used to it. He writes: "In the sea floor, unearthly creatures called garden eels anchored their tails in the sand as they fed on plankton suspended in the water. When I got too close they disappeared, like a mirage in a blue-and-white sea." National Geographic Society.

"At 15 feet, I found the squid. I watched them hunting. Fifteen inches long, they would hang like little zeppelins, their silvery spotlight eyes catching every movement in the rocks below them. Then they would tilt downward, tentacles first, and begin to move imperceptibly toward their prey." David Doubilet.

Sunrise. Cape Hatteras, North Carolina, USA. © **David Muench**

Moonrise. Hope Bay, Antarctic Peninsula. © **Patricio Robles Gil**/Sierra Madre

"The sun and the moon are born and die at sea. That is how big it is." Italian proverb.

Mother polar bear with cubs. Wapusk National Park, Manitoba, Canada.

© **Thomas D. Mangelsen**

Mother polar bear with cub. Wapusk National Park, Manitoba, Canada.

© **Thomas D. Mangelsen**

The great ice bear was thought to wander across the immense Arctic, over the frozen sea. Scientific studies have shown, however, that these animals belong to geographically discrete populations that move following seasonal and established patterns.

Atlantic spotted dolphins. Bahama Islands.
© **Chuck Davis**

"...the concept of working closely with friendly wild dolphins was a new one for me. [...] We learned quickly, the dolphins call all the shots. When they want to interact with humans, they show up and do so. [...] The dolphins seemed to be much more interested in me when I would hold my breath and dive and swim with them." Chuck Davis.

Magnificent sea anemone and hard corals.
Papua New Guinea. © **Mike Bacon**

"The magenta or purple color of the pedal disc of this magnificent sea anemone tucked amongst the hard corals with the clarity of the water and the silhouettes of overhanging trees with clouds above added another dimension to the photograph." Mike Bacon.

West Indian manatees. Crystal River, Florida, USA.
© **Mike Bacon**

West Indian manatee. Florida, USA.
© **Birgitte Wilms**

"In the islands they call Windward, namely Cuba, Hispaniola, Puerto Rico, and Jamaica, is found what is called a manatee, a strange type of fish, if the name fish can be applied to an animal that gives birth to its young live, and has teats and milk with which it nourishes them, and grazes on grass in the fields..."
Joseph de Acosta.

Pages 232-233
King penguins. Salisbury Plains, South Georgia Island, UK.
© **John Shaw**

"Be fruitful, multiply, and in the Seas / and Lakes
and running Streams the waters fill; / and let the Fowle
be multiply'd on the Earth." John Milton.

Humpback whale flukes. Inside Passage, Alaska, USA.
© **John Hyde**/Wild Things

Humpback whales. Inside Passage, Alaska, USA.
© **John Hyde**/Wild Things

"If, as a photographer, I had to choose just one subject to
portray, it would be whales. The rhythms of the sea and
the mysteries that continue to surround the lives of whales
are irresistible to me." John Hyde.

Greater flamingo. Inagua Island, Bahama Islands.
© **Gerry Ellis**/ENP Images

Greater flamingos. Ría Celestún, Yucatán Peninsula, Mexico.
© **Patricio Robles Gil**/Sierra Madre

Flamingos, unique birds due to their peculiar appearance and coloring, as well as their ability to endure difficult climatic conditions, are very gregarious, and constitute one of the oldest bird families on Earth. Their capacity for travelling across great distances sometimes allows us to observe the spectacle of a flock of flamingos many kilometers out to sea.

Fin whale. Gulf of California, Mexico.

© **Flip Nicklin**/Minden Pictures

Brown pelican. Boomers Beach, La Jolla, California, USA.

© **Richard Herrmann**

"We know now what was unknown to all the preceding caravan of generations: that men are only fellow-voyagers with other creatures in the odyssey of evolution. This new knowledge should have given us, by time, a sense of kinship with fellow-creatures; a wish to live and let live; a sense of wonder over the magnitude and duration of the biotic enterprise." Aldo Leopold.

Thayer's gull. Canadian Arctic.
© **Joe Galkowski**

"[...] these congregations of waters were called sea
and as they are many, there are,
of necessity, many seas."
Joseph de Acosta.